North Wales Tramways

Keith Turner

DAVID & CHARLES
Newton Abbot London North Pomfret (Vt)

for Su

British Library Cataloguing in Publication Data

Turner, Keith
North Wales tramways.
1. Street-railroads – Wales, North – History
I. Title
388.4'6'094291 HE4718.W/

ISBN 0–7153–7769–8

Library of Congress Catalog Card Number: 78–74089

Photoset and printed in Great Britain
by Redwood Burn Limited, Trowbridge & Esher
for David & Charles (Publishers) Limited
Brunel House Newton Abbot Devon

Published in the United States of America
by David & Charles Inc
North Pomfret Vermont 05053 USA

Contents

Acknowledgements

For their help in locating and supplying material and information I should like to express my gratitude to the librarians and staff of the following libraries: Llandudno, Wrexham, University College of North Wales Bangor and Cambridge. Similar thanks are also extended to the archivists and staff of the then Caernarvonshire and Denbighshire records offices.

Individual thanks are given to Pat and Nigel Woods, who helped to make it all possible, and to Gary Bowen for his photographic assistance. I am especially indebted to Mr Richard Jones for much valuable information relating to the Pwllheli tramways; to the chairman of the Llandudno Tramway Society, Mr Stuart A. Rivers of 34 Madoc Street, Llandudno for similar information on the L & CBER; to Mr Tony Hurst for the loan of the P & L tickets; and to Mr D. W. K. Jones of Effingham House, Hartswood, Reigate, Surrey for the photographs of the L & CBER: he will gladly supply copies of these on request.

Finally, a special mention must go to Su who gave me so much time, help and encouragement along the way. If not for her, it would never have been written. And to anyone who assisted in any way, and has inadvertently been omitted from this list, my sincere apologies and thanks.

Introduction

The history of the narrow gauge railways of North Wales has provided the subject matter for many books and innumerable articles but still the coverage is not complete, still the list of publications increases annually. By comparison the tramways of North Wales have been virtually ignored, judging by the criterion of the printed word. A quick glance at the bibliography given at the end of this volume will readily bear out this sad truth. What *has* appeared in print has been almost solely confined to only two lines – the two most famous lines – to the virtual exclusion of all others. This book is an attempt to remedy the situation in as complete and balanced a manner as possible.

Though rich (as will be seen) in ideas, projects and grandiose schemes, North Wales managed to produce only six distinct and separate tramways of any degree of permanence (and even then one was virtually a rebuild of a predecessor), none of which could even remotely claim the title of a system. The longest never reached more than 8½ miles, the shortest less than 900yd. What they lacked in length or complexity however they amply made up for in that vague abstract one can only call 'character'; character they certainly possessed. They ranged from urban and industrial to rural and sea-fringed settings; they catered for both everyday transport needs and recreational outings; their passengers varied from an early morning huddle of coal miners on the one hand to a solitary corpse journeying to its last resting place on the other. And always in between were the swarms of pleasure-bent trippers and holidaymakers.

Like their more famous neighbours, all six tramways were narrow gauge lines; three of them were of 3ft 6in. This same gauge was coincidently that adopted by the Nantlle Railway in mid-Caernarvonshire, opened in 1828. Some time soon after the opening of this line a passenger service was commenced with one or more horse-drawn vehicles, thus achieving for the line the distinction of being the first rail passenger service operator in North Wales. This line was not however a tramway but a tramroad, built for the conveyance of slate from quarry to port and worked by horses. Nor can the Snowdon Mountain Tramroad (as it then was), opened in 1896, be classified as a tramway: it was a rack railway. The only true tramways constructed in North Wales are the six that provide the bulk of the subject matter of this book and the short-lived one mentioned in the final chapter; those others dealt with in the last chapter are included because they come closer to the category of 'tramway' than that of 'railway' and are therefore described for the sake of completeness (they might otherwise be in danger of being overlooked) as well as for their own inherent interest.

1 Wrexham – horse

WREXHAM AND DISTRICT

In the nineteenth century, as indeed today, the east Denbighshire town of Wrexham was an important focal point for its surrounding area, and for several centuries had been the market town of the district. In this it was ideally placed being on the edge of the agricultural land to the east and the industrial development to the north, west and south. One of the most important commodities dealt in on market days was horses, bred and reared in the country for uses in the collieries and other industries. Since the beginning of the Industrial Revolution, coal had been worked in the area, and later steelworking had developed (notably at Brymbo to the west), together with lead mining and brick and tile works. This mineral wealth had in fact been known and worked in some degree from Roman times.

Rail transport was a common feature of the early industrial workings and, not surprisingly, Wrexham became a railway centre of some importance as rival companies vied with each other to capture the mineral and other freight traffic. In 1849 the Shrewsbury & Chester Railway (promoted as the North Wales Mineral Railway) opened with a station at Wrexham; five years later it was absorbed by the Great Western as part of its main line to Chester. The station, on the north side of the town, was named General. In 1866 came the Wrexham, Mold & Connahs Quay Railway which ran north for ten miles from Wrexham to Buckley to meet the Buckley Railway which connected with the London & North Western main line to Holyhead at Connahs Quay. The WM & CQ station was sited beside Wrexham General and called Exchange. In 1887 the line was extended under the GWR line and into the town with a second station, Wrexham Central. In 1895 the nominally independent Wrexham & Ellesmere Railway opened from Central Station to Ellesmere, providing a link with the Cambrian Railways there. The GWR had meanwhile constructed a branch to Brymbo and the LNWR one to Mold; the WM & CQ was taken over by the Great Central and the W & E by the Cambrian. The last branch to open was on 30 October 1901 when the GWR opened its line south to Rhos. By doing so it (unsuccessfully) attempted to capture the traffic carried from there to Wrexham by a single-track horse tramway.

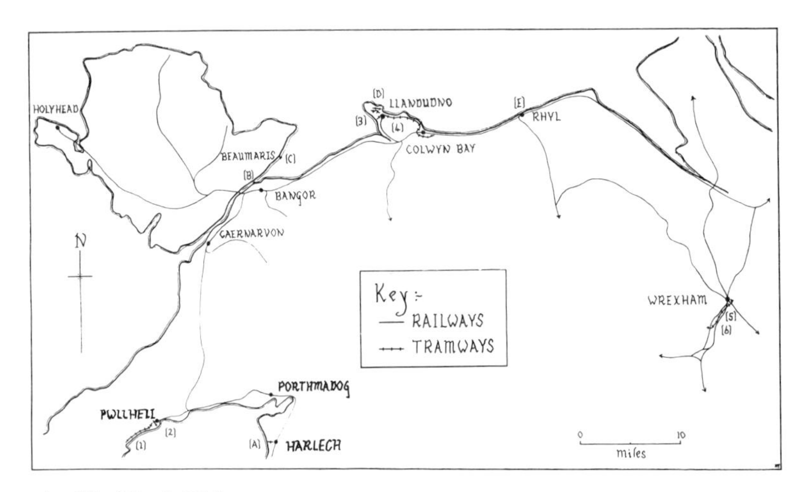

1 The North Wales tramways:

Principal tramways:
1: Pwllheli & Llanbedrog Tramway
2: Pwllheli Corporation Tramways
3: Great Orme Tramway
4: Llandudno & Colwyn Bay Electric Railway
5: Wrexham District Tramways
6: Wrexham & District Electric Tramways

Minor tramways:
A: Harlech Tramway
B: Bangor Pier Tramway
C: Beaumaris Pier Tramway
D: Great Orme Cabinlift
E: Voryd Park Miniature Tramway

But to go back thirty years: the area south of the town was an important coal mining district and thus offered several attractions to any prospective tramway company, including the transport of workers from Wrexham and the conveyance of the inhabitants of the village of Rhos (officially named Rhosllanerchrugog but usually abbreviated) to Wrexham for everyday business. Coupling this with the picture of the hordes of country folk streaming into market up the Ruabon road from the south – people who could doubtless be induced to ride for much of their journey on a tramway – the idea soon found concrete support.

A TRAMWAY IS PROMOTED

To obtain authorisation for a tramway to serve the district a parliamentary bill was promoted and eventually passed on 16 June 1873 as the Wrexham District Tramways Act. This authorised the incorporation of a company to be known as the Wrexham District Tramways Co and gave the necessary powers to construct a series of 3ft gauge tramways between Wrexham and Rhos. The first was to commence in Ruabon Road, Wrexham, and travel in a south-westerly direction for a distance of 2 miles 62.7 chains to the New Inn at Johnstown, a tiny hamlet to the east of Rhos on the Wrexham-Ruabon turnpike. From here a short extension was to travel westwards for 12.35 chains to Rhos. Both tramways were to be single track though a loop was provided for on the first line outside the Black Lion at Rhostyllen, roughly halfway between Wrexham and Johnstown. The other three tramways authorised, again all single track, were to run through the streets of Wrexham from the end of the main tramway to the toll gate at the end of Regent Street marking the beginning of the Wrexham-Mold turnpike. No part of the system was to open until it had been inspected and passed by the Board of Trade.

The Wrexham District Tramways Co was permitted to raise capital amounting to £10,000 in £10 shares; twenty shares was the minimum qualification for a director, of which there were to be five. The first directors of the new company were listed in the Act as Thomas Barnes, the Hon George Thomas Kenyon and William Low, plus two others to be nominated by them. The company, in addition to building the tramways, was also to lease the toll rights and powers of the Wrexham-Mold turnpike from the Trustees of the Wrexham & Mold Turnpike Road from 1 January 1874 for the sum of £760, spread over a period of three years.

OPEN, LET, SOLD AND CLOSED

The tramway opened for goods and passenger traffic on 1 November 1876 and ran from the New Inn at Johnstown as far as the cemetery in Ruabon Road, Wrexham, on the edge of the town. This was the site of a toll gate and it was not until this was removed after a month that the trams continued for another $\frac{1}{4}$ mile to the final terminus at the junction with Ruthin Road. The depot was sited at the Johnstown terminus and housed the line's solitary single-deck car. It soon transpired that one

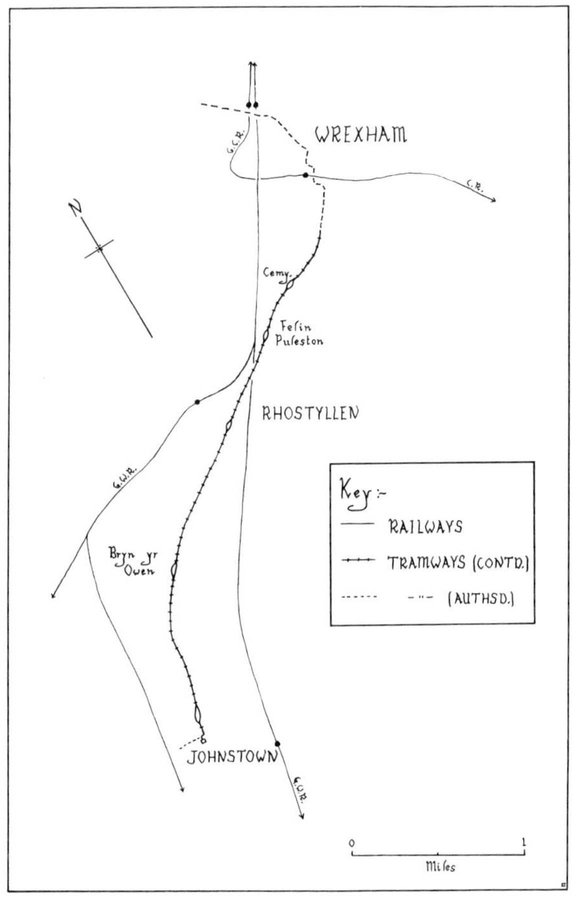

2 Wrexham horse tramway

vehicle was not sufficient to cater for the potential traffic (the one car took 1½ hours to complete a round trip to Wrexham and back) and a second car, a double-decker, was quickly ordered. So that a staggered service could be operated and long waits avoided at Rhostyllen, a succession of passing loops were laid, one near the cemetery, one at Felin Puleston (Puleston Mill), one at Bryn yr Owen and one near the Johnstown terminus.

The use of horse traction over the line evidently left a lot to be desired for just two years after the tramway's opening the WDT Co applied to the Board of Trade for permission to use steam tramway locomotives. This was not yet permitted for regular services in Britain and the Board of Trade refused the request on the grounds that the condition of the roads over which the tramway ran were in no way suitable for locomotives. (The next year, 1879, an Act of Parliament was passed to allow steam working on street tramways but the Wrexham company felt it pointless to apply again since the Board of Trade would still have had to approve the request.) Thus rebuffed, and still in the days before the use of electric traction on tramways, the company was in something of a quandary. Horse working was slow and with only two cars making the leisurely journey, revenue was not all that it might have been. Also, the authorised extension to Rhos (it would have actually fallen far short of the village at the foot of a long hill) had not been constructed, possibly because all the company's capital had been exhausted, and this curtailment of the tramway system – the Wrexham extension never materialised either – was reflected in the company's change of name which took place at this time from the Wrexham District Tramways Co to Wrexham Tramways Ltd. The company furthermore decided to remove the burden of the line from its own shoulders and place it on someone else's and the tramway was offered out on lease.

In about 1880 a Wrexham coal merchant, Mr Frederick Llewelyn Jones of Vicarage Hill, took over the running of the line while the owning company bided its time until it seemed more attractive to resume the operation of the tramway itself. The lease was for £3 per week, the WT Co retaining ownership of both the track and the equipment. Eventually the company decided to sell the latter and Jones purchased the stud of six horses, the two cars and their associated trappings in June 1884 for the sum of £100. The enterprising coal merchant, naturally possessing a great deal of knowledge regarding the construction of horse-drawn vehicles, thereupon set to work and built a third car for the tramway. It was another double-deck car and was constructed in Jones' yard in Abbott Street. Unfortunately it was too tall to pass under the archway out into the street when completed, and consequently the top deck had to be removed and replaced outside. When all had been made good Jones gave a luncheon for the mayor of Wrexham to mark the momentous occasion!

On 24 August 1885 Jones paid the tramway company half of the £100 for the stock and appears to have hung on to the other £50 until 3 March 1890, in spite of several demanding letters from Mr Bevan, secretary to the tramway company. Notwithstanding this dispute Jones continued to run the line, presumably profitably, in return for £3 per week rent until 25 April 1896 when the figure was changed to £200 per annum instead, renewable every year.

In 1898 Wrexham Tramways Ltd was approached in a potential take-over bid by the Drake & Gorham Electric Power & Traction Co Ltd – the name was an obvious portent of what was about to happen to the line. While Jones' trams continued to follow the plodding horses along the muddy roads plans were being made to modernise the tramway, even replacing it entirely if need be. On 10 December 1898 the company gave notice that it intended, under the Tramways Act of 1870, to introduce electric traction. This move had been authorised by a Provisional Order of the Board of Trade permitting the take-over of the old company, the construction of additional tramways and the substitution of new track for the old. The Provisional Order was confirmed by Act of Parliament as the Wrexham District Tramways Order on 9 August 1899. Under this Order Wrexham Tramways Ltd was empowered to relay and electrify the whole of the horse tramway route, construct a 48 chain extension southwards from Johnstown towards Ruabon, extend the line at the other end for a distance of 76 chains through Wrexham and out onto the Mold turnpike and construct an 18.2 chain branch from the town centre down Hope Street and High Street.

Excluding the Wrexham branch, the new tramway would stretch for a total distance of 4 miles 6.6 chains of which 42.5 chains were to be double track. The permitted gauge could be up to 3ft 6in. After one year Wrexham Tramways Ltd was allowed to sell out to the Drake & Gorham Electric Power & Traction Co. On 22 December 1900 the D & GEP & T Co, under the auspices of the National Electric Traction Co, sold its interest in the tramway to a concern which was at that time busy building up its own tramway empire – the British Electric Traction Co. The BET set up a subsidary company to take control of the running of the line, as was its policy, and thus the Wrexham & District Electric Tramways Co Ltd was formed. Registered 26 August 1901, the company had five directors: J. F. Albright (chairman), E. Garcke (soon replaced by C. L. Robertson), J. Devonshire (soon to leave), G. Cornwallis-Smith and J. V. Kitchener. The company's secretary was W. S. Wreathall and the registered office at Donington House, Norfolk Street, London WC. Nominal share capital was 10,000 £5 shares.

On 26 April of that same year the last horse tram had run over the line:

> On Friday the last journey of the Wrexham and Johnstown horse tram was made, and the work of preparing for a service of electric cars was immediately started. The cars, in addition will be brought through the principal streets of the town, and their advent is looked forward to with considerable interest. At present buses will run between Wrexham and Johnstown.
>
> (*Rhos Herald* 4 May 1901)

SERVICES AND STOCK

As is probably apparent from the above history of the tramway the line was operated with the minimum of stock and services.

Originally this was achieved by using just two horses and two tramcars with the unfortunate consequence that on the steeper sections of the line the passengers had to get out and walk – if not actually physically assist the labouring horse! Soon two more horses were added to the stock to be used as trace horses on the more difficult sections of the line; by the end of the tramway's life the stud had risen to a total of nine spread between three different stables at the New Inn, Bryn yr Owen Smithy and Felin Puleston.

Services

Like the horse stock, the number of journeys made daily appears to have increased over the years. At first only three or four round trips were made but this soon rose to seven. Only one car was needed for the basic service except on Thursdays and Saturdays (market days) and public holidays when the service was doubled by the introduction of a second car. The two cars would work from opposite ends of the line and pass at the Black Lion; the extra passing loops added later suggest that when traffic was heavy (especially in later years) all three cars were pressed into service.

In 1901 the first tram of the day left Johnstown at 8.30am and the last returned from Wrexham at 8.15pm. On Saturdays this was extended to 10.45pm.

Fares

Under the authorising Act of 1873 fares were limited to not more than 2d per mile though the company was not bound to charge less than 3d for any one journey. Accordingly the fares in force were 3d single (this was raised to 4d for a brief period but later lowered) and 5d return. The tramway was also empowered to carry cattle and goods of every shape, size and description. Each had its own rate but it seems unlikely that any freight – apart from the odd parcel – was ever handled as no facilities for its carriage existed.

Stock

Car No 1 was a single-deck vehicle fitted with toast-rack type seating, running on four wheels, with a fixed roof and side curtains to provide some form of weather protection. It could carry about twenty passengers. It was constructed for the opening of the line by the Starbuck Car & Wagon Co Ltd of Birkenhead, as was car No 2. This second vehicle, built shortly after the line's opening, was a double-deck car with knife-board seating on the open top. The bottom deck was completely enclosed; both decks held about twenty passengers. Communication between the decks was via a single staircase at one end. This (and the other end platform as well) was fitted with a large sheet iron screen, completely shielding the nearside of the platform – perhaps intended as a decency board. Again it was a four-wheel vehicle. Above the lower deck windows was the legend: WREXHAM–RHOSTYLLEN–SMITHY–JOHNSTOWN; below the windows was a large, centrally placed 2, below which was the legend: WREXHAM DISTRICT TRAMWAY. Livery was probably brown and cream, possibly originally lined.

Soon after the arrival of No 2 car No 1 was rebuilt as a copy of it by a local coachbuilder at a cost of £75.

Car No 3 was again a four-wheel double-deck vehicle, very similar to No 2. It was almost certainly a direct copy by Jones – possibly the truck too was copied or else it was purchased from Starbuck – and formed the last addition to the fleet. One slight difference between Nos 2 and 3 that can be seen in photographs is the arched, as opposed to flat, tops to the windows of the latter vehicle. Internal lighting was supplied by an oil lamp fixed to each bulkhead while externally a candle lamp hung from the canopy at either end. This was apparently the same for the other two cars for when Jones purchased the tramway stock he acquired, along with two French horns and a whip, some lamp snippers.

The fate of all three cars after the 1901 closure is unknown; presumably the metal work was sold for scrap and the bodies for sheds or outhouses as so often was the case.

2 Wrexham – electric

A NEW LINE

After the termination of Jones' horse-drawn service on the old tramway, horse buses were used as a replacement service by the W & DET Co while work forged ahead on replacing the track (to a gauge of 3ft 6in), constructing the extensions at each end and erecting the overhead wire. To widen the area served by the tramway a third extension was mooted – and authorised on 31 July 1902 by the Wrexham District Tramways (Extension) Act. This new line was to be a 51.59 chains branch from the former terminus at the New Inn, Johnstown, westwards along Maelor Road, up Gutter Hill and Hill Street, then northwards along Broad Street to Rhos High Street, thus serving that village directly. Of this branch 13.44 chains were to be single and the rest double track.

In 1902 also the old tram shed at Johnstown opposite the Red Lion in Maelor Road was demolished and the construction commenced of a new depot to house the fleet of electric cars. Measuring 100ft by 48ft it housed 5 shed roads, 3 of which were laid over inspection pits, together with the necessary offices, stores and so on. It was a brick building, erected by Messrs Jenkins & Jones, a local firm of builders' merchants and contractors (the partnership split soon afterwards to form two separate concerns), under the supervision of Ivor H. Jones. It was completed by 17 January 1903 according to the *Rhos Herald* of that date which described the structure as a 'magnificent building'. By this date five of the ten cars ordered from the Brush Electrical Engineering Co, Loughborough, had arrived and everything was ready for trial over the completed portion of the line. The trackwork had been installed by Dick, Kerr & Co Ltd of Preston, using 94lb grooved girder rails paved with granite setts, and was completed between Johnstown Depot and Wrexham General. The work had been done under the direction of

R. J. Howley, the permanent way engineer, A. J. Lawson, the BET's electrical engineer and W. J. Gale, the BET's resident engineer. Wiring was carried out by the BET; points, crossings and other special items of trackwork were supplied by Messrs Askham Bros & Wilson Ltd of Sheffield.

The date fixed for the official Board of Trade inspection was 1 February and the first trial trip over the completed section was arranged for Friday 23 January but it is doubtful whether this actually ran; the first publicised run took place three days later on the Monday. One car departed from Johnstown at 11.40am carrying a number of 'principal residents', several Wrexham Town Council and Rhos Parish Council members, Mr G. W. King, the W & DET manager (since November 1902), Mr Malpas the company's chief inspector and a handful of others. The car ran as far as the former horse tramway terminus in Wrexham only, and departed for the return trip at 1.20pm. The whole trial was reported as being 'very satisfactory'. The same newspaper report also carried the informed rumour that the GWR was to lower the fare to Wrexham from Johnstown still further.

There then began a rather exasperating (for the company) period of waiting for the Board of Trade inspection. The Board first of all put it back to 14 or 16 February (Saturday 14 February saw a second 'official' trial run over the line); then it was postponed to 4 March but once again called off at the last minute. Eventually it took place on 10 March:

> On Tuesday, Colonel Yorke, on behalf of the Board of Trade, made the final inspection of the electric tramway from Wrexham to Johnstown. Colonel Yorke went over the whole route, and made a careful inspection of everything connected with the tramway. A few minor details were pointed out for attention, but nothing to delay the trams running immediately.
>
> We understand that the continuation of the line from Johnstown to Rhos via Gutter Hill will be commenced in about three weeks' time.
>
> (*Rhos Herald* 14 March 1903)

With the 'few minor details' attended to the official opening took place on Saturday 4 April – after several weeks of conflicting rumours. The company could hardly have picked a better time, for the weekend was followed by Wrexham's annual fair on the Monday; on that day the trams ran from early in the morning right through to midnight and during the whole three days the cars were packed out.

> Crowds of people went to Wrexham on Saturday, Sunday, and Monday; and instead of walking or going by train, gave the new cars a trial. The cars gave every satisfaction as far as safety was concerned. Everything seemed as snug and as safe as a railway carriage. The speed too, was very swift when the cars were running; but when one had to stop several times in a loop, awaiting the arrival of another car, one had plenty of time for arguing and discussing the mystery of electricity. Except for these trifling delays, which, no doubt, will soon be rectified, the cars gave every satisfaction.
>
> (*Rhos Herald* 11 April 1903)

Electricity must indeed have been a mystery at the time to many for the tramway was the first in North Wales to use this new and strange form of traction. But it appears to have been quickly accepted and the future of the company seemed a very bright one.

COMPLETION

The final layout of the whole system was completed (with one small exception) soon after the opening. Within a matter of weeks the few hundred yards between Wrexham General and the northern terminus at the Turf Hotel was open. (The Turf Hotel on the Mold road took its name from the racecourse by it, later converted into a football ground; the inn sign changed but not the name.) At the southern end of the line the company encountered several obstacles to its Rhos extension which, when the tramway opened, had made no progress at all beyond the GWR level crossing at Johnstown. Work immediately began on

Page 19: A view which typifies the predominantly rural settings of the early North Wales tramways: W & DET No 8 between Wrexham and Johnstown, 1903.

the branch, coinciding with the opening of the tramway, with the covering of old drains on Gutter Hill and the widening of the top section of the road to provide a sufficient passageway for the trams. By mid-June 1903 this work was all but finished and the track had been laid across the GWR on the level at the foot of the hill. The next section up Gutter Hill to the beginning of Hill Street was completed on Sunday 30 July, ready for a Board of Trade inspection.

That was as far as the Rhos line ever reached. The rest of 1903 was taken up with a protracted dispute between Mr Henry Dennis, of New Hall, Ruabon, and Mr W. L. Brenthall, the W & DET secretary. The subject of the dispute was Dennis' claim to possess absolute ownership of the roadway over which the track had to pass; no agreement could be reached after lengthy negotiations and the matter was let drop with much ill-feeling. In the words of the *Rhos Herald* of 5 December 1903, 'from facts which have recently been brought to our notice it is improbable that the company will ever consent to again negotiate with Mr Dennis'.

The truncated branch opened in 1904 and was known as the Rhos branch though in reality it served the district of Ponciau. A connection was laid later in the year to enable cars from Rhos to run onto the Ruabon extension without having to reverse. (This triangular junction at Johnstown was also used to turn cars periodically to equalise wear.) The Ruabon extension reached just a few hundred yards past the New Inn (the limit of the 1899 authorisation was 48 chains) close to Hafod Colliery. From the New Inn the line assumed the route of the old horse tramway for the 3 miles to the edge of Wrexham, running for practically the whole of this distance through a rural landscape. The only small settlement passed was at Rhostyllen before the straggling outskirts of Wrexham were met. The first passing loop was at Fynnant Road, then they occurred at the waterworks (Bryn yr Owen Smithy), Church Street Rhostyllen, Tesless Rhostyllen, the cemetery (Empress Road) and the Oak Tree, just before the end of the horse tramway route. Proceeding into Wrexham the next loop was in Pen y Bryn Road shortly before the single track doubled to wind through the town centre

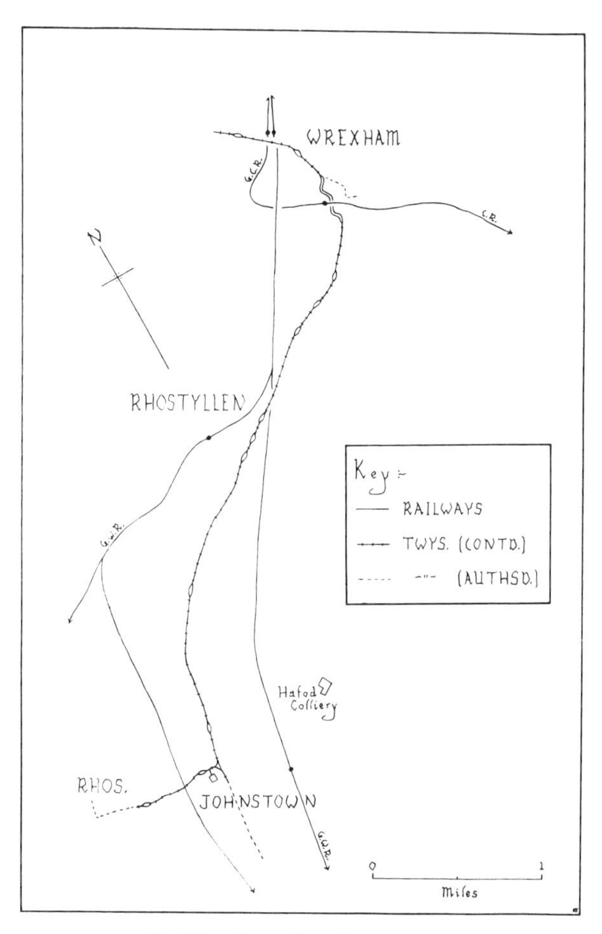

3 Wrexham electric tramway

(passing under the GCR) via Vicarage Hill (the 4 chains stretch of 1 in 12 here was the steepest on the line) and Hill Street (where the track was interlaced for 35yd). On reaching Regent Street it reverted to one track, passed over the GWR and the GCR by the General and Exchange Stations before arriving at the Turf Hotel. The only major track alteration still to be executed was the installation of a third passing loop at Rhostyllen, outside the Black Lion, in 1920. This was despite continual rumours that extensions were to be constructed in Wrexham, to Brymbo and beyond, and to Llangollen via Ruabon.

The overhead wires – 0 gauge copper – were carried on bracket arms on side poles (31ft high in Wrexham and 30ft elsewhere) and were fed with 550V from the corporation's power station (opened originally for lighting purposes in 1901). This was supplied under a 21 year contract made in 1903 – a contract which was later to hasten the tramway's closure when it expired in 1924.

King – formerly of the Potteries Tramways, another BET line – died in office in 1906 and was replaced by Mr A. A. Hawkins from the Greenock & Port Glasgow Tramways (again a BET system); Hawkins remained with the company right through to the closure. Legend has it that the late manager was taken to Wrexham Cemetery by tram; this is very likely for in 1909 driver W. Edwards was accorded a 'tramway funeral' and perhaps the trams were used as hearses on other occasions, especially from Johnstown or Rhos. The tramway had its share of other incidents to upset the normal pattern of events during its lifetime. One of these was the constant danger of flooding of certain sections in the country, interrupting normal services. On such occasions passengers were conveyed between the trams which halted on each side of the affected section in horse-drawn vehicles. Sometimes flooding was more widespread and resulted, as happened in the October of 1903, in the disruption of electricity supplies. Some of the country sections were also liable to subside because of mining operations carried out beneath them and in such cases the relaid stretch of track would be tarred, rather than paved with setts, to facilitate any later repairs.

As on any other comparable tramway undertaking minor incidents involving the line were numerous and staff seemed to appear in the law courts with monotonous regularity. In 1903 alone three such occasions deserve mention. In June, Shadrach Griffiths, a local carrier, sued the W & DET Co for £8 in respect of damage to his trap. The accident had been caused by a tram frightening the horse at night, causing it to back the trap into the tram, throwing those in the trap out, fortunately without injury. Despite the fact that the driver had noticed the horse to be rather restless, foreseen an accident and pulled up, despite the

Page 23: (above) Early 1903 interior view of the newly-constructed W & DET depot at Johnstown. Note the original Tidswell lifeguards and the variety of indicated destinations on the cars; *(below)* W & DET No 8 crossing the River Clywedog at Felin Puleston, 1903.

fact that the tram was in fact *stationary* when the trap hit it, despite all this the judge obviously regarded these new-fangled things with the gravest displeasure and awarded the damages, making the inane comment that:

> Electric tram cars were a recent introduction to the district, and horses were not all accustomed to them. The easiest and simplest way for the company to avoid such accidents in the future would be for the driver to stop.
>
> (*North Wales Chronicle* 27 June 1903)

The company could never have won!

In October a Ponciau labourer was convicted of assaulting J. D. Mackie, one of the tram drivers, while drunk and in December Oscar Clint, a Swede and ex-tram conductor, was fined 10s 6d (52½p) plus costs for embezzlement. Clint had played the traditional tram and bus game of collecting fares but issuing no tickets once too often.

With the growth of population and settlement in the district, especially between Wrexham and Rhostyllen, the tramway flourished in the years before World War I – so much so in fact that the increase in traffic led to the tramway's eventual downfall, for the W & DET decided that it could profitably enlarge its scope and tap new areas of potential traffic, not with expensive capital outlay on new tramways but with the more modern, more flexible means of public transport – the motor bus.

A CHANGE OF NAME

On 23 September 1912 a Daimler CC type single-deck bus began operation in Wrexham for the tramway company, and others soon followed to work as far afield as Chester and Llangollen. It quickly became obvious to the company in which direction their progress should be and on 19 March 1914 the Wrexham & District Electric Tramways Co Ltd became the Wrexham & District Transport Co Ltd. At the outbreak of war however the Army requisitioned most of the company's bus chassis and the trams had a last, brief period of command of the roads. Fortunately all the trams had been completely overhauled and patched-up just before the war, for they were, without exception, in a shocking structural condition.

After the war the buses returned to the roads of Wrexham and its neighbourhood, their numbers swelled by those of several rival concerns, and virtually the only regular passengers on the trams were the grimy colliers after bus services commenced over the tramway route. The age of the tramway's expansion – if it could be called that – finally came to an end in 1920 when a small, two-road shed was built near the Turf Hotel to house the cars used on the short local service through Wrexham. The end was in sight though for this was purely an economy measure designed to save running costs and electricity.

CLOSURE

As the 1920s progressed so did bus services. Overheads were low – there was no track to keep up, no twenty-year-old vehicles to maintain. The trams were kept running, though they were nearly falling apart, for they still provided a revenue-earning service though it was plain to all those concerned as to what the eventual outcome would be. The first major blow came in 1924 when the company's contract with Wrexham Corporation for the supply of electricity expired. The corporation, not unnaturally, seized the opportunity to up the asking price for current and a new, yearly-renewable contract was drawn up. From then on the tramway company did its best to economise on current used and one by one the services were pruned, to be replaced by buses. At the end of March 1926 the colliers' services were the last to go leaving just the bare, basic service to the tramway. It only needed for a large item of expenditure to arise and the line was doomed.

The tramway was by now virtually dead on its feet anyway and at the end of 1926 notice was given of its closure. The service was further reduced until by March 1927 just two cars worked the line. Wrexham depot had already been turned over to the needs of the growing bus fleet. On 31 March the last two trams ran, Nos 2 and 9. The latter was used for the final service of the day, leaving the Turf Hotel at 11.10pm after a short ceremony. In the hands of driver Albert Davies it reached Rhos at 11.40pm and then travelled back light to the Johnstown depot to join its nine stablemates. The tramway days of Wrexham had finally ended; it is doubtful if anyone bothered to mourn their passing. The cars were kept for a while in the hope that they could be sold complete but no definite offers emerged and they were stripped of all useful parts, the bodies being sold locally for sheds, chicken runs and garden houses. In Wrexham the track was mainly covered over to form a smooth road surface while outside the town the county council removed the track and poles and sold them for scrap or building purposes. Johnstown depot went the way of that at Wrexham and became another bus garage.

In 1928 the Wrexham & District Transport Co was transferred to Tilling & British Automobile Traction and in 1930 amalgamated with the GWR road services to form the Western Transport Co Ltd. Three years later it was amalgamated with Crosville Motor Services Ltd which, though under different ownership, survives as the major bus operator in North Wales.

OPERATIONS

Working

As the major part of the line was single track the long sections between the various passing loops were a hazard to smooth operations. Surprisingly, no comprehensive system of signalling was ever provided, the tramway being worked instead with a variety of aids to ensure that no two trams met on a single track section. The first of these was simply that the timetable was so arranged to enable trams to pass at the different loops – this naturally entailed long delays on occasions and much inconvenience to the waiting passengers (a complaint first voiced on the tramway's opening day). The second aid was a system of board signals used when unscheduled services operated: a normal service tram would carry a square board hung on the dash to indicate to drivers waiting in the loops that either one tram (a black board) or two trams (a red board) were following. The latter signal soon disappeared from use, rarely being needed, as did the former with the run-down of services. The third aid to safe working was a red signal lamp each side of the Johnstown level crossing. When used these were operated by the crossing keeper but were rather superfluous since the tram driver, like any other road user, could see whether or not the gates were against him; consequently their use was soon abandoned. The last working aid was a white signal lamp at the top of Pen y Bryn which was lit to indicate to north-bound trams that a car was climbing the steep hill out of Wrexham.

Various procedures also had to be observed by tram drivers, both in the interests of safety and in the interests of the company. Before descending a hill the car had to be brought to a halt and an application of the track brake made; this prevented any headlong dashes that might have got out of control and also tested the brake to ensure that it was functioning properly. While running every effort had to be made by the driver to conserve electricity as an economy measure (a consumption meter was fitted to each car) and this resulted in either very slow crawls or else fast bursts of speed followed by long periods of coasting – neither method hardly conducive to the comfort of the passengers!

Services

Before the tramway opened it was announced that the public service would be at 25 minute intervals, except on Mondays when it would be 10 minutes and Saturdays when it would be 8 minutes – both these enhanced services coming into force at 10.00am. The service would commence with an early morning workmen's car from Johnstown at 4.45am and from Wrexham at 5.15am. A Sunday service would start at 10.00am.

The actual commencing service was little different from that envisaged. Normal services began at 8.30am from Johnstown and ended with the 11.00pm from Wrexham; the early morning workmen's tram left the Rhos terminus for the Hafod Colliery at 5.00am and thence to Rhostyllen for the colliery there. Others followed, one travelling right through to Wrexham and back for the benefit of workers from there or anyone wishing to catch an early train from the town. The general public service ran from Rhos to Wrexham, by-passing the Ruabon extension, with trams leaving each terminus at 30 minute intervals (possibly more frequent or with double workings on Mondays and Saturdays); the Sunday service commenced at 9.30am and was the cause of much controversy in the district. (The issue of Sunday running was to appear elsewhere in North Wales with regard to tramways.) The basic argument was between the tramway company and those who wished to use the tramway (or see it used, usually for their benefit) on the one hand and the individuals and bodies who regarded Sunday running as a violation of the Sabbath on the other. The matter of Sunday observance was a strongly-held principle of the chapel sects of North Wales. One of the bodies to voice a definite opinion was Rhos Parish Council, only to be put firmly in its place by the tramway company:

Dear Sir,

SUNDAY RUNNING

My Directors have now carefully considered the views of your Council expressed in your letter of the 11th inst. [June 1903] with regard to the running of our trams on Sundays. I am instructed to state that in view of the large number of the residents in your district who have availed themselves of the facilities afforded by our trams on Sundays, they cannot see their way to discontinue the service. My Directors feel sure that the adoption of such a course as you suggest would be considered a public inconvenience by a large majority of the population.

We have made enquiries locally, and find that the little drunkenness which there is in the district has in no way increased by reason of the service of cars which we now run on Sunday, and moreover, we are informed that drink can be obtained without going beyond the three mile limit [a regulation for the benefit of bona fide travellers].

I might venture to point out to your Council that some little time ago we were asked to run trams at an earlier hour on Sundays in order to enable people to use them as a means of going to Divine worship, and that steps have been taken to meet this request.

Yours faithfully,

THE WREXHAM & DISTRICT ELECTRIC TRAMWAYS, LTD.

Another representation to the company was more fruitful. Shortly after opening Wrexham Town Council complained about the 30 minute service through the town and requested some improvement. The result was the introduction of a local service from Turf Hotel to the cemetery, again at 30 minute intervals but staggered with the Rhos service to provide a tram through Wrexham every 15 minutes in each direction. After World War I this was improved further to a 10 minute service and in addition every half-hour one of these 'locals' ran through to the Black Lion at Rhostyllen where the new loop had been constructed. By 1926 this service had reverted to one car just serving Wrexham.

Fare and tickets

Before 1920 the ordinary fare over the tramway was 3d single and 4½d return. The distance was divided into four 1d stages for pricing shorter journeys. (This was in accordance with the 1899 Act which laid down a maximum charge of 1d per mile or fraction thereof.) For a short period a system was tried using ¼ mile stages at ¼d per stage but it was not a great success and was soon dropped. For use on the workmen's trams only, a workman's return ticket cost 1d. In 1920 the company was allowed to raise the standard fare to 4d, with five 1d stages, and the workman's return to 1½d.

Bell punch tickets were issued on the trams by the conductor for normal services; workmen (and schoolchildren) could purchase their special weekly Edmondson tickets from Johnstown depot.

STOCK

The tramway fleet comprised ten passenger cars and two service vehicles. By January 1903 five of the passenger cars had arrived; the remaining seven vehicles came by 14 February, well in time for the opening.

Nos 1–10

The passenger cars were manufactured for the tramway by Brush to a standard double-deck design. All 10 were identical and seated 22 on the lower, enclosed deck and 26 on the upper, open deck; the decks were linked by reverse stairways. Overall dimensions were: length 27ft 8in; width 6ft 6in; height 9ft 9in. The length of the saloon was 16ft 0in. The body was of wooden construction and was mounted on a 4-wheel Brush type A truck (with 30in wheels on a 6ft wheelbase) powered by 2 GE58 motors. The controllers were BTH B2 pattern.

As constructed the cars were equipped with Tidswell automatic wire-mesh lifeguards, Leather's patent ventilators and electric communication bells. Soon after entering service, however, the lifeguards were replaced by sturdier wooden ones of a slatted type and the bells disconnected. Two further interesting and somewhat advanced features were a portable telephone handset which could be plugged into the nearest feeder pillar to contact the depot if need be, and a trolley retriever spool attached to the dash to control the trolley rope. Four braking systems were fitted: an ordinary rachet, an emergency rheostatic (controller) operating via the motors, a slipper brake (lever) operating on the wheels and a track brake bearing on the rails. This latter brake was, according to contemporary sources, fitted on the cars as supplied and was not therefore later added at the instigation of the Board of Trade as some accounts have suggested. It consisted of a 30in long shoe bearing directly onto the rails and was powerful enough to lift the car off the ground. Known as the 'Spencer electric skotch' brake after its inventor – the manager of the Halifax tramways – it was needed because of the steepness of Vicarage Hill in Wrexham.

Livery was red and cream with gold lining. The car number

was in gold on each side of the central electric headlamp in the end dashes. The BET magnet and wheel device was painted in the centre of the waist panels; apart from this no other identification marks were used, in accordance with BET standard practice. At various times advertisements were carried on the trams which were often liberally festooned with them. At the ends of the top deck were mounted illuminated destination indicators; interior lighting was by ten electric fittings. Oil signal lamps were carried in case of emergency.

The service cars

The tramway's two service vehicles were a salt wagon and a tower wagon. The former was a 4-wheel truck which was towed behind a car along the line in icy conditions and from which salt would be sprinkled onto the track; the latter was a horse-drawn vehicle used for inspecting or repairing the overhead wire. The horse was hired whenever needed.

In the early 1970s a Wrexham group of enthusiasts located and obtained the body of car No 6 for preservation.

3 Pwllheli & Llanbedrog Tramway

S. ANDREWS & SON

The second horse tramway to appear in North Wales (apart from the short-lived Harlech Tramway for which see Chapter 9) was in complete contrast to the first in as many ways as could be possible. It would be misleading to say that it was *built* as a tramway; a more appropriate word would be *evolved*. Its evolution and growth were inseparable from those of Pwllheli as a coastal resort and was the direct product of the imagination and enterprise of a Cardiff firm by the name of Solomon Andrews & Son. Although originating from, and based in, Cardiff, Andrews & Son had extended its property development and building interests to other parts of Wales, notably along the Cambrian coast, and in addition operated horse buses in Cardiff (and also in other Welsh and English cities). On the south side of the Mawddach estuary across the river from Barmouth the firm had already constructed and worked horse tramroads to convey building materials from quarry to railway; passengers were also carried for a short while. In short, S. Andrews & Son was a very diverse concern with many different, but complimentary, interests. It is therefore not surprising to discover that all these interests came together at Pwllheli in a unique fashion.

By the 1880s Pwllheli was a moribund little town, consisting of a few narrow streets huddled behind a large harbour on the southern shore of the Lleyn peninsular (or more correctly, simply Lleyn). The town lived on memories of past glories, of the days when the harbour was a hive of activity and the port prosperous. Now the harbour was full of silt, shallow and useless, and the town had to look in other directions in order to survive. The most obvious one was towards the sea – excellent beaches were to be found just ¼ mile beyond the harbour. All that was needed was a large development programme and a good publicity campaign. The Cambrian Railways' winding and beautiful line up the coast of Cardigan Bay reached its terminus in Pwllheli in 1867 but it was not until 1888 that a start was made on the development of the town as a resort with the construction of a very short promenade on what was known as the South Beach. Only a hundred yards or so long it had sand dunes to its left and sand dunes to its right and was reached from the town by a very poor road indeed. A solitary block of houses and the South Beach Hotel completed the scene. It was a start – of sorts – but the real impetus to the whole scheme came in 1894 when S. Andrews & Son decided to take a very real interest in the future of the town. In that year Andrews constructed, a few hundred yards west of the South Beach Promenade, a longer parade in the dunes and began to build houses and a hotel upon it. He purchased all the necessary land for the project and it quickly became apparent that this area of development, named the West End, was to be the focal point for trippers and holiday-makers in the town.

To supply what stone was needed for the work Andrews developed a quarry at Carreg y Defaid, a rock outcrop 1¼ miles to the west along the shore. From here to the West End was laid a narrow gauge horse-worked railway or tramroad; from the West End to Pwllheli proper a new road was constructed across the rough ground. This took the name Cardiff Road and provided the only link between the two areas of settlement. Behind the new buildings along the promenade Andrews laid out a recreation ground, the first in Pwllheli, which quickly became famous throughout North Wales. It was equipped with a good football pitch, lawn tennis courts and a concrete cycle track; special tournaments and events were frequently held during the summer season. During the construction of the recreation ground, sidings were laid from the mineral line to carry stone right into it. With the construction programme at the West End completed for the present the tramroad had outlived its original purpose but, obviously realising its potential, Andrews set about converting it into a horse tramway for holiday-makers.

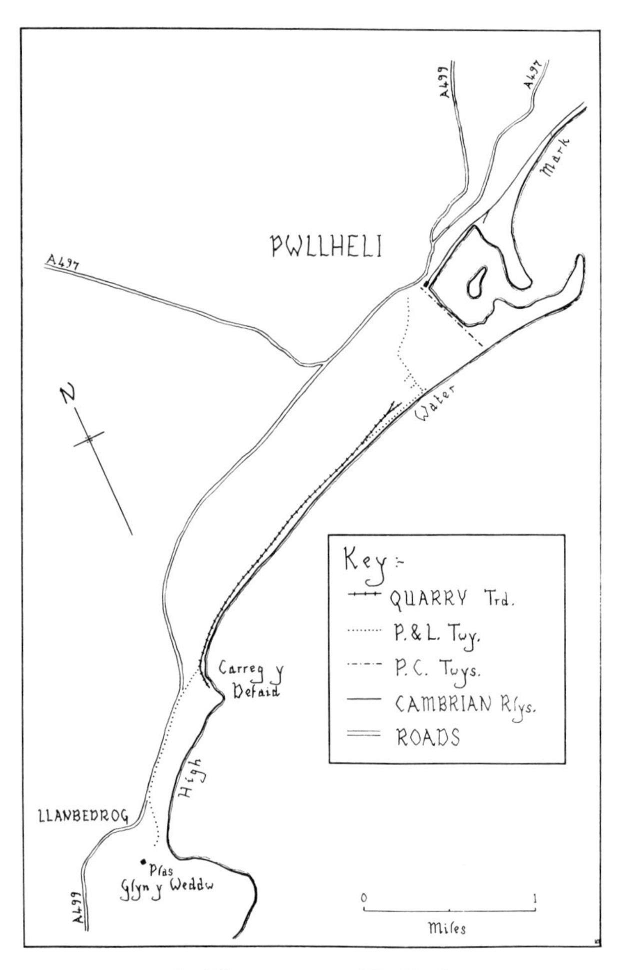

4 The tramways of Pwllheli

THE WEST END TRAMWAY

The conversion of the tramroad would not have involved any major effort; it is more than likely that very little alteration at all was made to the track which consisted of flat-bottom rails spiked to wooden sleepers. The gauge was 3 ft 0in. The 'conversion' was carried out early in 1896 and the tramway appears to have been opened to the public on 1 August of that year. A surviving public notice announces a comprehensive service to begin on that date though a detailed search of the local press gives no mention of any opening ceremony – or indeed of the fact that the tramway was actually opened. The first passing mention of the line occurs two months later for on Wednesday 14 October the coast was hit by a severe gale during the night and the early hours of the following morning. The result was widespread damage and flooding in Pwllheli and havoc at the West End which had caught the full fury of the storm; nearly the whole of the 'Tramway to Carreg Defaid being dislodged or otherwise damaged' (*North Wales Chronicle* 17 October 1896).

The tramway at this time was known simply as the West End Tramway. The plans for it had been deposited with the Board of Trade at the end of 1895 (a £35 deposit fee was paid on 20 December) together with an application for a Provisional Order to construct the line. The total incidental costs of obtaining the Order amounted to £111 13s 4d (£111.66½). From the West End a connecting horse bus service ran along Cardiff Road to the town and from there onto the Cambrian Railways station on the far side of Pwllheli.

GLYN Y WEDDW HALL

In 1896 the opportunity presented itself to Andrews to expand his interests still further and, consequently, bring in more profits. The property known as Glyn y Weddw Hall, or Plas Glyn y Weddw, came up for auction. This was a large mansion complete with fifty acres of spacious landscaped grounds in the tiny village of Llanbedrog, 3¼ miles west along the coast from the West End. It had been built as a dower house by Lady Love-Jones, the widow of Gen Sir Love Jones-Parry KH of Madryn Castle and one-time MP for Caernarvonshire. After the death of his widow it was auctioned in the Madryn Estate sale in September 1896 and bought by Andrews for £7,000. He stated that his intention was to convert it into an art gallery and erect a permanent building in the grounds for horticultural shows. Other attractions were to be added, all designed to make it an attractive place to spend an afternoon. Complete with monkey house, it was a Victorian forerunner of the modern stately home concept! A collection of over 400 paintings and drawings, including many from the hands of the masters, was assembled and work began on converting the hall for its new role.

The manager of the West End Tramway, Mr F. E. Young, was also appointed manager of the hall and under his direction the conversion was carried out. When finished it included a roller skating rink and large tearooms. Meanwhile the obvious step of extending the tramway to the village of Llanbedrog was being taken together with a second extension, this time in the other direction into the centre of Pwllheli.

ALONG THE BAY

Unfortunately for the historian there is no record of precisely when the completed line opened to the public. The *North Wales Chronicle* of Saturday 31 July 1897 records the fact that it was open by then for it mentions the 'finest Art Gallery in Wales' at Glyn y Weddw Hall

> at the far end of the beach which is reached by a newly constructed marine tramway, running for a distance of four miles along the sand banks overlooking Cardigan Bay.

The report went on to state that the hall had recently joined the other attractions of Pwllheli and a further item reported that it and the tramway had both been open the Thursday week previous. This pushes the probable date back to mid-July or earlier; another press report adds what could be strong evidence in favour of mid-July when the *Caernarvon & Denbigh Herald* of Friday 16 July noted that the old man himself, Solomon Andrews, had visited the town during the previous week and 'when he made his appearance on the "Maes" on Tuesday quite suddenly there came out hundreds of the inhabitants to give him three ringing cheers'. A reasonable supposition is that Andrews performed some sort of opening ceremony during this week. Two months later, on 30 September, he was rewarded for all he had done for Pwllheli with the freedom of the borough – the first to be conferred for the town.

The new tramway, now known as the Pwllheli & Llanbedrog

Tramway, commenced at the end of Cardiff Road where it joined Ala Road in the centre of Pwllheli. The terminus consisted of a short stretch of double track and a small wooden ticket office. From here the single line ran down Cardiff Road, through waste land (much as it still is today) to the built-up area at the West End. At this end of the line was a four-road shed and workshop complex, a short siding down Recreation Road to carry supplies to the recreation ground and a single track spur to the east on the promenade. This was the terminus for the 'town line' as it was called. The distance covered between Ala Road and the West End Parade was nearly $\frac{3}{4}$ mile. A turntable connection at the end of the line led into the tramway's depot and stables and a set of points connected with the two-track terminus of the former West End Tramway.

The line to Llanbedrog ran westwards from this junction as a single track along the promenade and carried straight on over the end of the road onto the sand dunes. At a point $\frac{1}{2}$ mile from its start, a point known as Talcymerau-uchaf, a branch from the recreation ground converged with the main line. It continued along the sea shore for another $1\frac{1}{2}$ miles before reaching Carreg y Defaid where the old quarry line veered off to the left. The main line turned slightly inland, climbing steeply, and joined the Pwllheli-Llanbedrog road which it accompanied on the seaward side (though several hundred yards from the shore) until just beyond the 3 mile point when it turned southwards away from the road to make its own way to its terminus between the village and the sea. Here two long tracks formed the layout with two wooden buildings and a platform comprising the station. In later years a large tram body of unknown origin was added to the waiting room facilities. A little way on from the railed-off station was the village church of St Pedrog and a little way on from that the entrance to Glyn y Weddw.

All along the line from the West End to Llanbedrog was a multitude of passing loops and sidings, one loop roughly every 250yd. These loops and sidings were not necessarily permanent and many were laid only to be taken up again after a few years. No real record exists of the actual precise track plan at any one date other than that shown on contemporary Ordnance Survey

WEST END TRAMWAYS, PWLLHELI.

2½ MILES ALONG THE "UNRIVALLED SOUTH BEACH."

On and after August 1st, 1896, the above Trams will leave the West End Hotel and Careg-y-defaid as under, weather permitting, until further notice :---

Leaves West End Hotel.		Leaves Carreg-y-Defaid.	
9 0 a.m.	4 0 p.m.	9 20 a.m.	4 20 p.m.
9 40 a.m.	4 20 p.m.	10 0 a.m.	4 40 p.m.
10 20 a.m.	4 40 p.m.	10 40 a.m.	5 0 p.m.
11 0 a.m.	5 0 p.m.	11 20 a.m.	5 20 p.m.
11 40 a.m.	5 20 p.m.	12 0 n'n.	5 40 p.m.
12 20 p.m.	5 40 p.m.	12 40 p.m.	6 0 p.m.
1 0 p.m.	6 0 p.m.	1 20 p.m.	6 20 p.m.
1 40 p.m.	6 20 p.m.	2 0 p.m.	6 40 p.m.
2 0 p.m.	6 40 p.m.	2 20 p.m.	7 0 p.m.
2 20 p.m.	7 0 p.m.	2 40 p.m.	7 20 p.m.
2 40 p.m.	7 20 p.m.	3 0 p.m.	7 40 p.m.
3 0 p.m.	7 40 p.m.	3 20 p.m.	8 0 p.m.
3 20 p.m.	8 0 p.m.	3 40 p.m.	8 20 p.m.
3 40 p.m.	8 20 p.m.	4 0 p.m.	8 40 p.m.

Fares : 2d. each way.

Omnibuses, in connection with the above Tramways, will run from West End Hotel to Town and Station, and vice versa.

Fares :—{West End Hotel to Town, 1d. / Town to Station, 1d.} and vice versa.

S. ANDREWS & SON,
PROPRIETORS.

Office :—CARDIFF ROAD.

—TO LET,—

For Concerts, &c., West End Assembly Rooms.

Seat, 450. Terms : Apply—T. CUNNINGHAM, Cardiff Road.

Printed by Owen Humphreys, 47, High Street, Pwllheli.

5 The first published P & L (West End Tramway) timetable

maps – maps that can be several years out of date. For this reason these loops and minor sidings are not shown on the accompanying map. By the time of World War I several more major changes had taken place; all lines to the recreation ground had been lifted, their period of usefulness over, the termini, depot, workshop and passing loop on the town line had been remodelled (see plan). After these alterations had been carried out no more were undertaken and the line remained as it was for the rest of its life.

6 Contemporary humorous postcard depicting the P & L

Like the Wrexham District Tramways, little factual evidence exists with regard to the history of the P & L between its opening and closure; what information there is is almost solely confined to the operational details of the line. A few sources do however shed some illumination on the picture. The stables and depot on the West End Parade were enlarged during 1898, for Pwllheli Borough Council minutes for 28 July of that year make mention of a dispute with Andrews & Son over the siting of the building. The council ordered it to be constructed in line with the West End Hotel (ie not project onto the promenade) but this was apparently not strictly complied with for the minutes of the council meeting of 27 November record a resolution to initiate proceedings for the removal of certain walls in front of the stables which were contravening the bye-laws. The matter seems to have been solved amicably for nothing more is heard of it, apart from a mention on 20 June 1899 that no action had been taken and the council was still waiting to hear from Andrews!

The P & L was undoubtedly popular, both with tourists and trippers in the summer and, just as important, the inhabitants of Lleyn in the winter – many of whom would walk from their village to Llanbedrog then ride into Pwllheli to do their shopping or business. In the summer season the main source of revenue came from organised parties of trippers, called at the turn of the century 'excursionists':

> Excursion. – On Tuesday about 600 excursionists arrived in the town from Harlech and the adjacent district, and proceeded to Glynweddw Recreation Grounds by tram, the catering being carried out by Messrs Solomon Andrew's staff to the satisfaction of all present.
>
> (*North Wales Chronicle* 1 July 1899)

The above item was typical of many in the local press. (Andrews is given incorrectly as Andrew's, a mistake often made elsewhere.)

Some though could never be satisfied, as this extract from a long letter to the *North Wales Chronicle* of 30 September 1899 shows. Mainly in fulsome praise of Pwllheli, the letter was signed 'an English Baronet' and posed the question:

> Could the proprietors make some regulations as to smoking on the cars by which means those who object to it would not be inconvenienced?

In 1900 a second dispute arose between Andrews and Pwllheli Borough Council. The council resolved on 20 April to ask for payment in respect of Andrews' tramway crossing Talcymerau Road which, claimed the council, did not belong to Andrews. No headway was made until October when Andrews agreed to pay an annual rent of 7s 6d (37½p) for crossing various roadways but in the following December altered the draft agreement, making it unacceptable to the council. On 20 June 1905 the council noted that a second line of rails had recently been laid in Talcymerau Road; the PBC thereupon demanded an extra 2s 6d (12½p) wayleave (so presumably the earlier disagreement had finally been settled) and requested that both lines be 'pitched and paved with setts'. Nothing had

Page 41: (top) Postcard showing the whole sweep of the P & L along the bay to the left, tram bodies, wheels and stone tipper waggons in the foreground, depot tracks on the right; *(Courtesy Gwasanaeth Archifau Gwynedd)*; *(centre)* a P & L high-sided open car poses for the cameras in Cardiff Road *(Courtesy Gwasanaeth Archifau Gwynedd)*; *(above)* Early view of the West End terminus with closed and open cars. The depot had not yet been built. Victoria Parade is beyond the dunes in the distance. *(Courtesy Gwasanaeth Archifau Gwynedd)*

been heard from Andrews by September and legal action was threatened. Andrews was by now an old hand at stringing the council along and sent a vague reply in October. The council promptly wrote back requesting a more satisfactory answer. For this they had to wait until January 1906! Andrews had at last agreed to pay the extra money; at the end of the year he was warned about the dangerous state of the roadway in Cardiff Road.

In view of the above altercations it will be seen that relations between Andrews & Son and the PBC were somewhat strained; by this date the council's own tramway was in serious difficulties – while Andrews' prospered – and the PBC's efforts to persuade Andrews to take over its own line met with a coldly polite refusal. (See Chapter 4 for further details.) When the council's tramway at last expired Andrews & Son kindly took the line's stock of three cars off the council's hands for a mere £50!

Just how long the P & L would have remained triumphant is difficult to judge; perhaps it might have survived right up to the present day as a tourist attraction, for it was already archaic by the 1920s. The question is purely academic for events were emphatically to dictate otherwise.

ENFORCED CLOSURE

During the night of Friday 28 October 1927 Lleyn was hit by a fierce gale, described as being the worst in living memory. Both the north and the south coasts of Caernarvonshire were victims of the destruction caused by wind, rain and sea. All round the peninsula widespread flooding occurred throughout the night, aided at Pwllheli by 50mph winds from the sea; the South Beach and West End promenades were inevitably the worst affected areas of the town. At the West End the sea wall was badly damaged but this was far from being the only casualty: 'The band stand on the West End Parade was completely destroyed and the old tramroad between Pwllheli and Llanbedrog was washed away by the sea' (*Caernarvon & Denbigh Herald*, 4 November 1927).

Laid along the sand dunes close to the high water mark for much of its length, the tramway was one of the first things to be damaged in the storm. About a $\frac{1}{4}$ mile of track on the Pwllheli side of Carreg y Defaid was completely and irrevocably washed away – along with the ground upon which it stood. Much of the rest of the coastal stretch was flooded, torn up or buried deep under sand and debris. Reconstruction posed a massive task, a task, sadly, dismissed as too expensive and impractical to execute. Besides, the trams could be replaced by buses capable of roaming further afield from Pwllheli. This decision was taken early in 1928 and the *Caernarvon & Denbigh Herald* of 2 March of that year wrote the tramway's brief epitaph:

> The owners of the Andrew's Estate have decided to close the well-known tramroad between Pwllheli and Llanbedrog, which was extensively damaged by the recent storms. Visitors to Pwllheli will miss the old-fashioned horse-drawn tramcar which ran along the foreshore for four miles.

At the same time, doubtless influenced by the fate of the PBC's short town line, the decision was made not to run the West End–Pwllheli section in isolation and all salvagable remains of the whole tramway were reclaimed in 1928. And so thirty-one years to the month after a storm greeted the birth of the P & L a storm killed it, leaving Douglas, Isle of Man, the sole exclusive operator of horse tramways in Britain. Who knows, they may yet return to Pwllheli.

WORKING THE P & L

Stock

Accurate details of the P & L's fleet of cars are not available and the following account has had to be compiled from the memories of the tramway's staff, travellers on the line and contemporary illustrations. Consequently there are several unavoidable gaps. Basically all were wooden, four-wheeled vehicles to which the horse's harness was attached, at either end, by a pole and chains. There were three different types of car, two being open and the third closed.

The first open design consisted of a flat frame upon which were mounted seven bench seats in toast rack fashion. The wooden seats, which held five persons each, had swing-over backs to enable passengers to face the direction of travel. Entry was via a running board which ran the length of the car on both sides, there being no sides at all to the car above the floor. The running boards were also used by the conductor to pass along while collecting fares. Used solely during the summer on the Llanbedrog line, the number of these trams is estimated at ten.

The second design of open tram appears to have had a similar frame and running gear but was fitted with low sides which came to just above seat level. Between these were again seven rows of seats, again of reversible wooden design, with the addition of a centre gangway for the conductor. The pattern was thus split into fourteen separate seats, each holding two passengers. These cars were used primarily on the town line (with the provision of sides they were safer in town traffic) and numbered five. (It should be borne in mind that these figures are by no means definite and represent the tramway's total stock used during its history rather than that existing at any one time.) Neither type of open tram had seats for the driver but merely a brake wheel or lever, depending on the car, at each end.

The closed design of tram had a saloon body, six windows on each side, seating about twenty-four passengers on longitudinal seats under the windows, a platform for the driver at both ends (complete with seat) and an overall vestibule roof. Interior illumination was supplied by oil lamps. Access was via the driver's platforms through sliding doors; in wet weather the driver would sit inside and hold the reins with the door slightly ajar! It is thought that there were up to six of these vehicles though possibly this figure is too high. They were used on both lines, exclusively so in the winter.

One of the tramway's vehicles deserves special mention. This was known as the 'tent car' on account of its appearance: judging from photographs it seems to have been an open car (probably converted from one of those described above) with the addition of a roof canopy and canvas side screens. It was used in the winter and on wet days and apart from the fact that it definitely existed little else is known about it. The builder of the trams is not known; possibly they were constructed by Andrews & Son or by a coachbuilding firm. The livery was believed to be red.

The other three cars owned by the P & L were those purchased in 1921 from Pwllheli Borough Council (see Chapter 4). Possibly they are included in the stock totals given above.

Services

The first public timetable, issued in 1896 for the original West End Tramway, shows a 20 minute service. With the opening of the extension to Llanbedrog this was altered to one departure every half hour. During the summer months trams often ran in pairs, one following close behind the other to avoid confusion at the passing loops, and six or more trams would be on the line at once. The points (and the track in general for that matter) were not always in the condition they ought to have been in and derailments were an accepted feature of the journey. On such occasions everyone would alight and the more able-bodied passengers would then hoist the tram back onto the rails. It is recalled that neither driver nor conductor would take part in these proceedings! On Bank Holidays and the like half-a-dozen trams would congregate at Llanbedrog in the evening and, bursting at the seams, return to Pwllheli in exuberant procession.

The town line, always operated separately from the coastal section, was worked by two cars in the summer and one in the winter. As on the Llanbedrog line, the trams stopped en route on request to pick up or set down passengers.

Fares

On the West End Tramway a fare of 2d each way was charged. By 1902 the return fare to Llanbedrog plus admission to Glyn y Weddw was 1s (5p); admission only was 6d (2½p). For parties of fifty or more the return fare plus admission charge included tea in the refreshment rooms. The single fare was 4d, return 8d (3½p). Sometime between 1910 and 1920 the return fare increased to 9d (4p) and the combined return and admission 1s

2d (6p). By 1920 the combined ticket cost 1s 4d (6½p). Children under twelve travelled half-price. The Post Office (on the Cardiff Road-Ala Road corner) to West End fare was always 1d each way and passengers for Llanbedrog had to buy a new ticket on the other line.

Tickets could also be purchased in advance; with an eye on the excursionist traffic they were available much further afield, as is indicated by this quote from a 1901 newspaper advertisement: 'Through tickets issued at reduced rates from all stations on Cambrian Railway'.

4 Pwllheli Corporation Tramways

THE COUNCIL'S TRAMWAY

The success of Andrews' tramway did not go unnoticed; other developments were also taking place in, or being planned for, the town – this time by the corporation. It therefore came as little surprise to anyone when at the borough council meeting on 13 September 1898 Councillor John Williams proposed:

> That the necessary application be made for powers to construct a tramway on the Embankment and that further consideration of the matter be referred to the Special Committee appointed to consider the Harbour question.

The proposal was seconded by S. W. Griffith and carried. The Embankment referred to was the road directly connecting the town with the South Beach Promenade; the improvement of this highway was then being debated. The matter was not raised again until 10 January of the following year when the Embankment widening scheme, including the provision of a tramway, was agreed to by the council. Tenders were immediately invited with the stipulation that the work would have to be completed within four months. At a meeting on the last day of the month the six tenders that had been received were opened; they ranged from £3,520 down to £1,199. Thereupon the borough surveyor submitted *his* tender for the sum of £933, adding that any extra work would not exceed the sum of £50. This tender was thereupon accepted – an inevitable decision, for Pwllheli Borough Council was in a very poor financial position and, throughout this period, continually had to borrow money. The eventual cost was to be £1,209 11s 2d (£1,209.56).

On 16 May 1899 it was decided to send the surveyor to Blackburn to inspect some second-hand tramcars available for sale and to appoint a special committee to consider the purchase of the necessary horses; the idea of working the line by electricity was apparently never considered, even in later years, because of

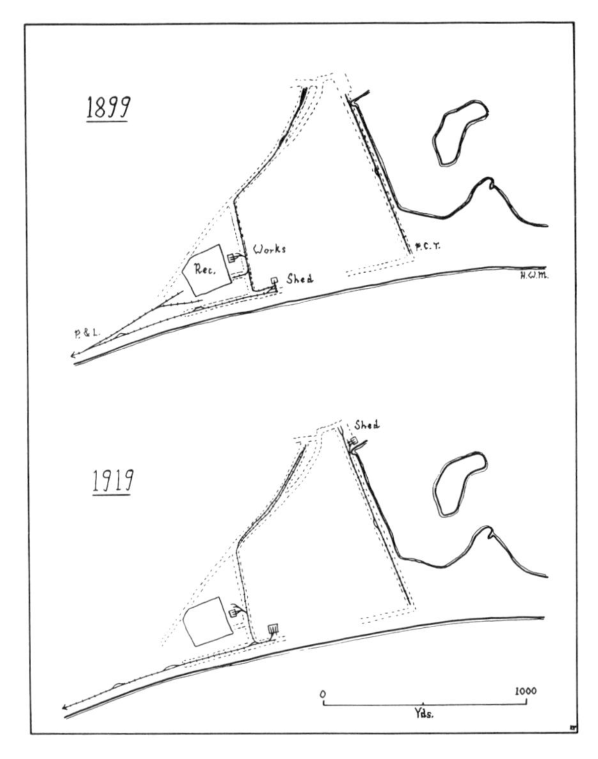

7 Pwllheli street tramway plans: see text for street names

the shortness of the line and the lack of the capital needed for such an undertaking. The idea of buying the Blackburn cars was abandoned for an unknown reason and instead the council called for tenders and designs. It is doubtful whether in fact the surveyor ever actually visited Blackburn for the next official decision taken was on 6 June when the designs received were discussed:

it was resolved that one open car at £38.10.0 [£38.50] and a closed car at £67 in accordance with the designs be bought from the Midland Railway Carriage & Waggon Company Shrewsbury provided that the former be delivered by the 1st July and the latter by 1st August.

(PBC Minutes 6 June 1899)

It was also resolved at the meeting 'that the Surveyor be authorised to get the closed tramway car to open at alternate ends'; that they should be lettered: 'Corporation Tramways. To and from Victoria Parade' (alias South Beach Promenade) and that the Hon F. G. Wynn, a local dignitary and landowner, be invited to open the tramway. The tramway, incidentally, was always officially referred to as 'the tramways' since it was regarded as merely the first of several.

Progress continued on all aspects of preparing the 2ft 6in gauge line for the opening later that summer. The special committee set up to purchase the horses delegated two members to travel to Ireland to buy a pair; one member flatly refused to make the journey! On 18 July it was decided to engage two stalls for the horses in Hunter's stables in Ala Road 'for the present'. The surveyor meanwhile, instructed by the Watch Committee, submitted his plan for a tramway shed, the erection of which was proposed for the town end of the line. The cost was put at under £30 for the whole work and it was resolved to let the contract on tender. The surveyor was further requested 'to include in the scheme Sanitary requirements and conveniences' and, with a view towards providing more permanent accommodation for the horses, recommended to design a corporation stable. While this was being done Mr Hunter's offer to let two stalls to the council 'at 2/6 [12½p] per week and manure' was accepted. The tender of Mr W. James Jones of the High Street for supplying two sets of harness for £6 10s (£6.50) was also accepted and a driver and conductor were advertised for in the *Udganu Rhyddid*, a local periodical. Applicants were invited to 'state the wages expected'.

The Hon F. G. Wynn having declined the honour of opening the tramway (as had the council's second choice, Colonel

J. Lloyd Evans), it was decided that the Mayor, Alderman William Anthony, would be asked to perform the ceremony. He promptly agreed and the opening date was set for Monday 24 July. The *North Wales Chronicle* reported:

> The Pwllheli tramway from the bridge to the South Beach was formally opened, on Monday, when over a thousand tickets were issued. Alderman R. O. Jones secured the first ticket, a feature which, locally, caused a great amount of interest, as naturally there was considerable rivalry among the leading inhabitants of the town in securing this memento of one of the many modern improvements of the enterprising schemes recently introduced by the Corporation.

The report went on to state that the town to South Beach line was just the portion of the intended system so far completed and that the mayor, ex-mayor, town clerk and several members of the council all made the trip along the line.

TO AND FROM VICTORIA PARADE

At the next council meeting after the official opening, on 15 August, the surveyor was instructed to prepare plans for stables for the horses to be located by the slaughterhouse and it was announced that Thomas Williams had been engaged as tram driver for 18s (90p) a week and Richard Jones as conductor for 6s (30p). Mr Elias Roberts was appointed to take charge of the horses for 12s (60p) a week. Three tenders for the tram shed and waiting room had been received, ranging from £139 16s (£139.80) to £103 9s (£103.45). The lowest of these, from Messrs Jones & Jones was thereupon accepted. It was then discovered that Jones & Jones were apparently so eager to get the contract that they had submitted another tender, this time for only £69 10s (£69.50). This was promptly accepted in place of the original offer with the proviso that only the waiting room was to be built at present. The work was to be carried out in three weeks with a 10s (50p) per day penalty for late completion.

In August 1899 G. Cornelius Roberts was appointed to superintend the running of the tramway at a wage of 5s (25p) a week and a special tramway committee of three appointed. This committee quickly amalgamated with the Roads Committee and together were responsible for all recommendations made throughout the tramway's life. The following month the committee suggested that a second driver should be hired; at the end of October the tramway ceased operation for the winter.

Thus began the quiet history of the Pwllheli Corporation Tramways. Running during the summer months only it seems to have got off to a moderately successful start and the council was obviously quite content with running the line itself for in January 1901 the question of letting the line out on tender was raised, only to be deferred for the present. The next month, not only did the Roads & Tramways Committee recommend that the council operate the line again during the coming season but that also a third car should be purchased, of open design, together with two new bells for the present cars. In the same month the surveyor was instructed to put the tram shed into proper repair (a consequence of Messrs Jones & Jones' low tender?) and to procure estimates for an open car. The tenders were opened at the council meeting on 26 March 1901; one in particular was not entirely satisfactory for, according to the minutes, 'the Surveyor was instructed to write to the Midland Carriage & Railway Co [sic] calling their attention to the sum paid for open car in May 1899'. He was also told to 'procure sample chair for existing tram rail', some of the existing ones being in need of replacing – throughout the history of the tramway the standard of tracklaying and repairing was consistently poor.

The correspondence with the Midland Railway Carriage & Wagon Co proved fruitful for on 16 April a revised tender of £44 15s (£44.75) was accepted. The new car appears to have arrived in late June for at the beginning of July a new horse was ordered to join the existing stock of two. A new wing was added to the tram shed to house the extra car and a stableman appointed to look after the horses. A tender of £2 5s (£2.25) for

100 chairs had by this time been accepted from the local firm of Pickerings; these were probably stored until the winter months when all repairs were usually carried out. A quantity of granite chippings was also obtained from the neighbouring Gimblet Quarry (sited on Gimblet Rock just offshore from the harbour) for levelling the surface of the track – the roadway was bare earth at this date with possibly a few chippings to provide some sort of surface, though this state of affairs was later rectified with the purchase by the council of a tar boiler to commence a programme of road spraying. The season ended on 3 October and recommenced the following Easter Monday. On the re-opening day receipts totalled £1 1s 3d (£1.06) while expenses, including a hasty repair to the track, came to 16s 5d (82p).

The tramway continued its life in an uneventful fashion though the track persistently gave trouble. In March 1904 the surveyor's plan for relaying it entirely was rejected by the council and he was told merely to repair it for the season. That same year the idea of erecting a waiting room at the town end of the line was raised, only to be deferred. (From this one can only presume that Messrs Jones & Jones never in fact built a waiting room in 1899 or else it had been converted into something else.) After the close of the 1908 season the Roads & Tramways Committee discussed at length the possibility of extending the tramway to the West End to meet up with Andrews' line by the next season. The town clerk was instructed to investigate this possibility; in April he wrote to Andrews & Son 'pressing for their reply in view of the near approach of the summer season'. The ensuing reply was that nothing could be settled as yet but that Mr Emile Andrews would be in town very soon when the whole matter could be properly discussed. The mayor was deputed to meet him but no agreement emerged from the talks – a result hardly surprising in view of the somewhat strained relations between Andrews & Son and the council.

The extension to the West End having failed, a lesser one was proposed and eventually carried out. The idea dated from 29 May 1909 when the committee visited the town terminus and tram shed at Pen y Cob. They decided to remove the shed and re-erect it beside the line on the edge of a piece of waste land known as Spion Kop, adjoining the Rebecca Wharf at the edge of the harbour. The track would then be extended 50yd into the town and the whole line paved with tar. It was subsequently decided that laying a conventional siding into the shed on its new site would unnecessarily break-up the newly-laid road surface there so instead a turntable would be installed to provide access. At the same time a tender of £2 3s (£2.15) from Messrs Ravenhill for painting the shed exterior was accepted. As for the new extension, no definite council decision was taken for some time for the whole future of the existing line was by no means certain. Receipts fluctuated, money for improvements was always short, and urgent repairs were constantly deferred; the council once again began to entertain the idea of letting the line out on a lease.

In September 1909 Mr T. J. Williams of Bodawen wrote to the council asking permission to lease the tramway for three months in the 1910 season. It was agreed that he could do so but only on a one month's trial basis. The nominal fee required was 2s (10p) but it is not certain that the arrangement was actually carried out for in April 1910 advertisements were issued inviting tenders for the hire of the line. The attractiveness of this offer can best be illustrated by the fact that no applications were received. The nominal fee quoted above was perhaps more than realistic! So the council was resigned to running the line itself for the season though it still had one hope left: it resolved to write to Andrews & Son to inquire whether or not 'they are prepared to consider their taking over the driving of the tram in conjunction with their own tramway'. They were most decidedly not. The surveyor's estimate of £22 for the tramway extension was also turned down, after considerable discussion.

During the 1910 season occurred what appears to be the only recorded accident caused by the tramway; the nature of the incident was in keeping with the line. On 14 June a bicycle belonging to Mr William Williams of Efailnewydd was damaged by one of the tram horses; his claim for compensation was eventually settled for £1 12s (£1.60). In June the go-ahead was at long last given to the town extension and by the council meeting of 25 July the work had been completed. One small event that occurred during the season is worth recording for it shows just how desperate the council was even for the odd few pennies; a party of eight visitors from Criccieth rode on the tramway without paying, claiming as an excuse later that they thought they had been covered by their tickets for the Pwllheli & Llanbedrog Tramway. The town clerk was told to press for payment.

At the start of the 1912 season seats were provided – after a long period of complaints – at the town terminus which, as a result of the 1911 census arrangements, was sited in the area now known as Station Square. It took its name from the new Cambrian Railways station which had been opened on 19 July 1909; the ½ mile railway extension from the old station (now the goods depot) had been made possible by the reconstruction of Pwllheli harbour, alongside which the railway could now run into the centre of the town. At the front of the station the 'square' was simply the end of Embankment Road where the new tram terminus was. Receipts for that year were considerably lower than usual as a result of very bad weather for the summer; before the line re-opened for the next season more repairs (including some rail relaying) took place. The next year work started on a scheme to link the South Beach Promenade with the West End Parade with a promenade road at a cost of £3–4,000.

By 1916 it was plain that the piecemeal policy of track repairs would have to be abandoned if the line was to be brought into a fit state for continued running, and on 29 February of that year it was resolved 'that enquiries be made with regard to the cost of purchasing and of *hiring* rails'. (My italics.) Almost inevitably the cost was found to be too great for the council's liking (even for second-hand rails) and any decision on the matter was postponed until the following year. Meanwhile the question of whether or not the trams could still run had to be faced. Typically this too was postponed, then postponed again, until on 30 May it was decided to run the tramway as usual from 1 July! In that year a policy was taken out with the Scottish Insurance Co to cover claims by the public against the tramway (a move doubtless inspired by the poor condition of the track) and receipts improved considerably over the previous year (£63 from 10 July to 16 September compared with £57 for ten days longer in 1915).

In 1917 T. J. Williams once again requested permission to run the tramway for the season and his offer was accepted on 31 July when the council resolved to let it to him at a nominal rent of 2s 6d (12½p) a week 'on his undertaking entire responsibility for the track and conveyances'. Williams operated the line for a five week season and again in 1918 when no-one else made a better offer – or indeed any offer at all in reply to the council's advertisements! Early in 1919 the council was told that if the line was to re-open, new or second-hand rails would *have* to be bought as the existing ones were simply not 'reliable'. Throughout those first months of 1919 the future of the line hung precariously in the balance. The cost of relaying the track with new rails and sleepers was estimated at £250, against which an offer had been received of £4 per ton for the old rails as scrap. (This would have realised £28 on the 7 tons involved.) The question of selling them was deferred for the moment and the possibility investigated of using some of them together with the minimum number of new ones; the long-suffering surveyor was instructed to look further into the possibility of obtaining some from a neighbouring quarry. These however were found to be unsuitable and so once again the bare minimum of repairs were ordered to enable the trams to limp along for one more season. It was to be the tramway's last.

THE END

In the autumn of 1919 some rails at Aberdaron were inspected but the price required was found to be too high; in February 1920 matters were put in hand to replace the trams with a 'motor conveyance'.

The council toyed with the idea of purchasing the necessary vehicle itself but decided in the end to invite tenders for the right of running a motor bus between the railway station, South Beach and the West End. In addition, on 30 March 1920:

> It was resolved that the existing rails be sold at the current market price subject to the condition that the purchaser must undertake the work of lifting the rails and on the understanding that the sleepers are left in their present position.
> (PBC Minutes 30 March 1920)

By the end of April one Mr Lock had paid £15 for a quantity of the rails. (The exact amount is not known but it was probably about half.) By the end of June an agreement had been reached with one Mr Ashworth whereby he was to run the replacement service from 9.00am to 9.00pm, at 15 minute intervals, from Station Square to South Beach (1½d) and South Beach to West End (1½d). Parcels were to be carried for 1d. Some delay was found in the inauguration of the bus service but Ashworth later promised to commence operations by 22 July. As for the trams themselves, all three were offered to Andrews & Son, together with the sleepers. The resultant offer of £50 for the cars was considered by the council to be too low; Andrews was apparently not interested in the sleepers. In September the cars were advertised for sale but no offers came; in April 1921 they were again advertised with exactly the same result. That March the surveyor was told to fill in the roadway where the track had been.

Andrews was again approached, the council indicating willingness to sell the cars for the £50 – an offer far better than the alternative of nothing! – and by 20 September they had been bought and removed from their shed. The shed and shelter were the object of several inquiries and proposals; in January 1922 it was eventually decided to lease the site to James Brothers Ltd who wished to erect a garage there. Subject to a suitable price being agreed, the shed and shelter were to be demolished. That autumn the last of the tram rails were lifted from Station Square and joined those which had been lifted from Embankment Road and stored in the hope that they might fulfil some other useful role in the future. So ended twenty years' life of the Pwllheli Corporation Tramways without it ever coming of age.

A SIMPLE OPERATION

Working the corporation tramway was simplicity itself. The number of cars owned (ie two to 1901 then three after that) equalled the maximum number of horses, drivers and conductors used to work the line. The horses were purchased at the beginning of each season and sold at the close (occasionally one would be kept over for the next year), often at a profit! The tram crews were engaged and dismissed in a similar fashion. The season started from 1 June or Whit Monday, whichever came first, and continued through to the last week in September or the first week in October; from 1915 onwards the normal starting date was put back to 1 July.

The actual line of the tramway was also simple. From Station Square it ran past the new depot, arrow-straight along Embankment Road to a point a few yards before the junction with Victoria Parade. It occupied the east side of the roadway next to the edge of the harbour (separated by a grass verge) which followed the tramway for almost the whole of its length. Apart from a short built-up stretch at each end the west side of Embankment Road consisted of waste ground. Roughly mid-way along the exactly ½ mile track was a passing loop in the middle of the road; at the depot a siding fed a turntable which in turn fed the two shed roads. The beach terminus was just a single track while the town end of the line boasted two roads. That was the whole of the track arrangement.

It seems that the line was so short that one car was sufficient to provide the normal service, though doubtless in peak holiday periods another would be called into action – hence the provision of the passing loop. In 1900 one horse and driver worked the tramway from 9.00am to 12 noon and from 3.00pm to 6.00pm, The second horse and driver worked from 12 noon to 3.00pm and from 6.00pm to 9.00pm, presumably with the same car. Only one conductor was needed, working from 9.00am to 9.00pm. During August the service was extended to 10.00pm.

About the cars themselves little is known apart from what has been mentioned before, one open and one closed car built in 1899 and one open car built in 1901, all from the Midland Rail-

Page 58: (above) This was the Pwllheli Corporation Tramways! Looking from Station Square, down Embankment Road, to Victoria Parade 1974; *(below)* The renovated PCT closed car body in its new role as an information kiosk in Station Square, 1974.

way Carriage & Wagon Co. All were four-wheeled vehicles hooked by two chains to a metal bar which in turn was linked to the horse's harness; at the terminus the chains were unhooked and the horse led round to the other end of the tram and hooked on there for the return journey. The two open cars were apparently no more than a platform with half-a-dozen swing-over bench seats mounted on it to allow passengers to face the direction of travel. The closed car was provided with two longitudinal seats, of plain slats, seating 8–10 in varying degrees of comfort. Access was by sliding doors at each end. The driver stood on a platform at either end of all the cars.

In the spring of 1908 the cars were cleaned and varnished; in 1915 they were again renovated. After their disposal to Andrews, and the subsequent closure of the P & L as recorded in the previous chapter, it is presumed that the running gear was removed for scrap and the bodies sold or destroyed. (The open car 'bodies' would no doubt have met the latter fate.) The closed car body did survive however and was rescued in 1969 by the PBC from a Lleyn farm where it humbly served as a chicken house. Now restored in green livery with white roof and cantrails and red window frames, it serves as an information kiosk outside the station.

FARES AND REVENUE

Fares and tickets

The fares charged on the tramway were first fixed on 18 July 1899 by the council at 1d each way. These were collected on the tram by the conductor. In addition pre-paid tickets could be purchased at 9d (4p) a dozen for the general use of the public; similar tickets were sold at 6d (2½p) a dozen for the sole use of workmen and quarrymen. The possibility of issuing season tickets was occasionally considered but always rejected by the council. In 1901 the idea of return tickets was also discussed but this too came to nothing.

In 1903 the issue began of pre-paid tickets at a cost of 1s (5p) for 24. These were presumably for the general public and workmen alike and were issued in an attempt to attract more custom. At the same time tickets were sold at 3d for 24 for the use of schoolchildren (though not after 5.30pm or on Saturdays). At an unknown date sometime after 1904 the cost of the pre-paid tickets was doubled to 1s (5p) for 12 and in 1919 it increased again to 1s 6d (7½p). The normal fare presumably increased in a proportionate manner.

The conductor-issued tickets were simply torn off a roll as required (no official mention was ever made of machines which were no doubt regarded as an expensive luxury!) while the pre-paid tickets were probably issued in booklet form. All were blank on the reverse until 1906 when Mr Caradog Evans, stationer, was given the right to advertise on the back of them in return for supplying them at half-price. In 1907 tenders were invited by the council from local tradesmen for advertisements on the tickets. By 1914 the space on the back was being let for the cost of printing the tickets.

Receipts and profits

Unfortunately the surviving records of the tramway's financial returns are very incomplete, to say the least, but it is possible to piece together some sort of overall picture. The most complete set of figures is that given below.

Year	*Receipts: £*	*Gross profit: £*	*Net profit: £*
1900	75		
1901	86		
1902	143		
1903	143	12	17 *loss*
1904	179	50	19
1905	258*	52	21
1906	240*	66	37
1907	132		
1908	132		

* These receipts include not only the fares collected but also the sale of the horses and the cost of work done for the road and sanitary departments. The net profit takes into account interest repayments on borrowed capital and depreciation.

The following break-downs of fares collected are the only two that exist.

Tickets	*1903*		*1904*	
1d roll	£102 11s 1d	(£102.55½)	£122 4s 4d	(£122.21½)
Schoolchildren	9s 0d	(45p)	15s 9d	(79p)
Pre-paid	£40 13s 0d	(£40.65)	£56 18s 0d	(£56.90)
Total	£143 13s 1d	(£143.65½)	£179 18s 1d	(£179.90½)

These give passenger figures, assuming all tickets were used, of 44,989 for 1903 and 58,146 for 1904.

After 1908 the receipts rose steadily until 1912 when they fell, soon dropping below the £100 mark. Profits never rose *above* this level. The fact that the council was prepared to lease it out, near the end of its life, at 2s 6d (12½p) per week shows clearly its value as a source of revenue!

5 The Great Orme Tramway

THE GREAT ORME

The Great Orme is without doubt the most distinctive feature of Llandudno; indeed, it once comprised its *only* distinctive feature before the modern town as it exists today was laid out. From the west, as far along the coast as Bangor, it appears to be an off-shore island rising abruptly from the sea and it only gives lie to this illusion as one approaches nearer. The Orme, as it is usually referred to, consists of a limestone mass some two miles long and one mile wide, rising to 679ft above the sea from which it rears so steeply and spectacularly on three sides. On the fourth side it is connected by a very low, very flat strip of land to the rest of the mainland to the south east. From pre-Roman times copper, and later lead, ore was mined here and from at least the sixth century a building has existed on the site of St Tudno's church on the comparatively level summit. The church gave its name to the parish (Llandudno meaning the Church of Tudno) and originally served the few miners' cottages huddled together on the landward slope of the Orme. As late as the mid-nineteenth century these and two small inns were the only habitations on the peninsula, then part of the estate of the Hon E. M. L. Mostyn, MP.

By this date North Wales was already becoming 'tourist conscious' and Mostyn realised that the rise of the fashionable watering place need by no means be confined solely to the south coast of England; with this in mind he began his grand scheme not only to build from scratch a complete resort but to then elevate it to a position in the north equal to that held by Brighton in the south. Accordingly in 1849 he offered and sold 176 plots of land on the low-lying peninsular; the scheme had taken its first steps towards becoming an unqualified success and fulfilling all of Mostyn's hopes. So sprang up the town that stands today, facing out to the east across Ormes Bay with the Great Orme on the left and its smaller namesake on the mainland, the Little Orme, to the right. With its broad promenade and majestic sweep of hotels and boarding houses along the bay it followed rigidly the pattern of its day, but in one respect it was unique – and that one respect was without doubt one of the principal reasons behind Llandudno's success: behind the town was *another* beach – a longer, wider, more desolate stretch of sand bordering the Conway estuary. This added attraction, together with the impressive majesty of the Great Orme, meant that the project could hardly fail. So Llandudno has grown to this day, purely residential, relying completely and utterly on its annual surfeit of holiday-makers to the total exclusion of any other form of industry (apart from the necessary services).

Promotions to add to the amenities of the town were rife and, naturally, the Orme figured in several. Walks and gardens were planned and executed on the lower slope and, in 1879, a toll road round the entire headland was opened for those visitors daring enough to walk or ride from east to west along the road that clung to the very edge of the rockface. Constructed at a cost of £14,000 the Marine Drive, as it was named, soon proved a most popular attraction and in 1897 the Urban District Council purchased the road from its private owners. It had now become evident that people prepared to pay to encircle the Orme would presumably also be prepared to pay to ascend it in comfort. Given added impetus by the pioneering efforts on a much grander scale of the Snaefell Mountain Tramway on the Isle of Man, opened in 1895, and the Snowdon Mountain Tramroad not so far from Llandudno, opened in 1896, the project to construct a tramway up the Great Orme began to take shape.

A TRAMWAY IS PROMOTED

The first funicular cliff railway in Britain had opened at Scarborough in 1876 and had soon been followed by others around the coast; shortly after this date the idea was put forward of installing a similar type of line up the Great Orme. Accordingly a group of local businessmen was formed to promote the scheme, engaging as consulting engineers Messrs Wood & Fowler of Liverpool. Their recommendation was the construction of a funicular railway to be worked in two separate sections since the total distance involved was too long for it to be safely worked as one line yet too short to justify the capital outlay and expenditure necessary for the adoption of any other

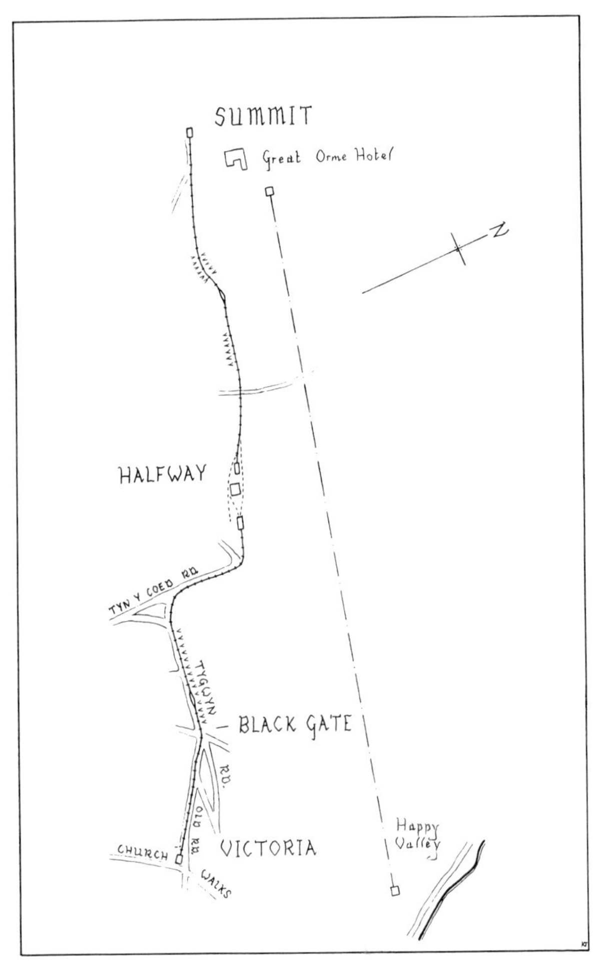

8 The Great Orme Tramway (left) and the Great Orme Cabinlift (right)

form of working. Notwithstanding this the projected line would be longer than any other funicular railway in Britain and – unique in Britain – would follow the continental practice of negotiating curves en route.

The next stage in the proceedings was to secure the necessary parliamentary approval for the scheme. Messrs R. S. Chamberlain & E. W. Johnson were secured as solicitors to the group of promotors and the Great Orme Tramways Bill was drawn up and introduced in Parliament during the 1897–8 session. At a meeting of the Llandudno Urban District Council in January 1898 it was agreed not to offer any opposition to the passage of the bill, the promotors having agreed to insert a special clause to give the council protection. A similar action was followed in respect to the Rt Hon Llewelyn Nevill Vaughan Baron Mostyn (the then Lord Mostyn), owner of the land through which the tramway would have to pass. The bill had an uneventful journey through Parliament and received the Royal Assent on 23 May 1898, passing into law as the Great Orme Tramways Act. Its full title was:

> An Act for incorporating the Great Orme Tramways Company and for authorising the Company to make and maintain a Tramway and Tramroad from Llandudno to or near the summit of the Great Ormeshead in the county of Carnarvon.

The authorisation had been given, according to the preamble, because 'the making and maintaining of a tramway and tramroad . . . would be of local and public advantage'. The GOT Co was authorised by the Act to raise capital of £25,000 in £5 shares with powers to borrow a further £6,250; the number of directors was given as five but the company was permitted to alter this figure between the limits of three and seven. Qualification for a directorship was the holding of at least 40 shares; the initial directors listed in the Act were Richard Conway, John Jones, Stephen Dunphy, James Lanham Mayger and George Alfred Humphreys. Richard Conway was later appointed chairman.

Permission was given to the GOT to construct two sections of tramway, the first being a single line of 3 furlongs 6.00 chains from a point in the yard adjoining Victoria House in Old Road, at its junction with Church Walks, up the Great Orme to a point near Penymynydd Uchaf farm house. The second tramway (described as a tramroad since it did not run along or beside a paved way) was to consist of a single line 4 furlongs 0.80 chains from the terminus of the first line to a point 110yd from the Telegraph public house near the summit. The gauge of both lines was to be 3ft 6in and the rails, in the roadway sections, were to be level with the road surface. The rails were in addition to be of a type approved by the Board of Trade (which was also to inspect both tramways before they could be allowed to open). The time allowed for the compulsory purchase of the land needed was two years with a further one year allowed for the completion of the works. The GOT Co was specifically forbidden to take (ie demolish) more than ten houses belonging to the 'labouring class' – these being defined as earning under 30s (£1.50) a week.

Powers were given to erect a hotel at the summit of the Orme by the tramway terminus, on the company's land, and also to erect offices, stations, waiting and refreshment rooms as need be. As regards the actual working of the line, this was left entirely up to the GOT Co with any form of animal or mechanical power permitted, subject to the approval of the Board of Trade. Steam working was, however, excluded from the possibilities, for the term 'mechanical power' was defined for the purposes of the Act as including 'electric and every other motive power not being steam or animal power'. If electric traction was adopted it was to be used with 'due regard to the telegraphic lines from time to time used or intended to be used by Her Majesty's Postmaster-General'. The Board of Trade was empowered to make any necessary byelaws to cover the use of mechanical power.

Other miscellaneous provisions were: the tramway was not to run on Sundays without the council's consent; Old Road from the King's Head to the Iron Gate was to be widened to at least 16ft by the company; a passing place for vehicular traffic was to be built between Plas Road and Tabor Hill; for the protection of Lord Mostyn all tracks and roadways incorporated into or destroyed by the construction of the line had to be replaced after completion of the tramway and all building plans had to be approved by him; no rolling stock was to be used that had been constructed for railway use; finally, there was a clause insisted upon by the council which is a veritable classic of its kind:

> The company shall make provision for the conveyance at a reasonable and fixed charge and in a decent and seemly manner of corpses for interment in the St. Tudno Cemetery.

CONSTRUCTION

Having expended some £4,000 on promotional expenses the newly-formed GOT Co was anxious to press ahead with raising its capital and acquiring the land needed. The process proved to be slow and quiet, though the *North Wales Chronicle* of 9 September 1899 mentioned that the company had purhased the Telegraph Inn and the adjacent land at the summit for the purpose of erecting a 'good hotel' there. A year later all the necessary land had been bought but construction had had to be delayed due to the fact that insufficient capital had as yet been raised. In October 1900 the company announced that it would still definitely go ahead with the scheme and by March of the following year only £4,000 was left to be subscribed. The company again announced that it was pressing ahead and that, according to the *Chronicle*, the line was to be worked on the 'tail rope' principle with a 'gas station' powering each section. The lower section was to be operational all the year round while the upper was to be worked during the summer season only. (The lower section was intended to serve the residential area on the lower slopes of the Orme as well as catering purely for holiday-makers.)

Construction eventually commenced in April 1901, the contract for the work having been awarded to R. J. Owen, a Llandudno firm of builders. (John Owen of this firm was one of the original promotors of the tramway and, together with Richard

Conway, served on Llandudno UDC; this and the fact that the other promotors were all local and influential men accounts for why so little official opposition was offered to the scheme.) This construction work had actually been sub-contracted by the main contractors, R. White & Sons of Widnes, who also supplied the permanent way materials and the winding gear under the supervision of their engineer, H. Enfield Taylor of Chester. As it transpired, the sub-contracting arrangement was not satisfactory and gave rise to a court action described later. The construction as a whole was directed by A. R. Ellison on behalf of the consulting engineers. The work began, logically enough, at the lower end of the route near the bottom of Old Road and advanced upwards. On 19 April the UDC agreed to close Old Road to vehicular traffic so that track laying could continue unimpeded in the narrow alleyway – for such was the state of the road at that date.

The first snag was immediately encountered: Old Road was so narrow that the track would unavoidably foul the water and gas mains below the surface. The GOT Co offered, in June, to pay £10 towards the £40 cost of new pipes as well as removing and replacing the old ones but in August the UDC stuck out for £20 – a very good bargain for the council since the pipes were at the end of their useful life anyway! As previously stated, under the terms of the 1898 Act Old Road had to be widened to at least 16ft and a passing place for other vehicles provided in the roadway between Plas Road and Tabor Hill. The latter had to be not less than 18ft long and 10ft wide. These provisions carried out, the line of rails emerged from Old Road and entered Tygwyn Road in June 1901. Just below the halfway point on the lower section, work on laying track halted and all hopes of operating the lower section of the line that summer were decisively dashed; the cable and rolling stock manufacturers were accordingly advised to delay delivery until the following year when the tramway would be in a better position to accommodate the equipment. More roadworks were required here; the road had to be widened to at least 23ft and a separate 3ft wide footpath laid; the tramway itself was to occupy a separate raised reservation on the right. There was also at this time a minor dispute with the UDC over some common land on the Orme, in the care of the ecclesiastical authorities, which had been leased to the GOT Co for a nominal sum (£10). The UDC was somewhat annoyed over this and tried to claim ownership with the obvious intention of extracting a much higher rent but was forced to admit defeat since the claim was invalid.

On 2 August the *Chronicle* reported:

> The construction of the Great Orme Tramroad is proceeding apace, and the work of laying down the rails is getting on most satisfactory. A portion of the tramroad may be expected to be in working order in about three weeks.

The report was optimistic for the steel cables were not in fact supplied by the St Helen's Cable Co until early May 1902 when each was hauled up to the halfway winding house by a team of twelve horses. The boilers for the steam-driven plant had previously been hauled up the Orme by a traction engine fitted with a winch; the traction engine had moved forward a short distance and then winched the boiler up to it before moving forward again. The process had then been repeated for the second boiler. On 23 May one cable was laid in the conduit which housed it on the paved lower section (see Chapter 6 for trackwork details) and linked to a car at the lower terminus. The car was then wound up to Halfway Station, let down and wound up again, apparently to the satisfaction of all concerned for exactly one week later the second cable was run out and attached to its car. The lower section was now ready for thorough testing before its Board of Trade inspection. Events were slightly behind schedule still, for at a meeting of the directors on 28 February 1902 it had been announced that the line would be opened sometime in May and that – with lofty ambition – the Prince of Wales himself (who would be in the vicinity on tour at the time) had been asked to perform the opening ceremony!

Meanwhile the GOT Co was busy searching for a manager for the tramway and in May offered the post to Mr A. Paton, an engineer, and the North Wales agent for the Liverpool & North Wales Steamship Co. He declined the offer. At the same time the company informed the council that it would not place advertisements on the carriage windows but would confine them to the interior woodwork. In mid-July the council gave the company permission to erect eight small direction signs on lampposts, on payment of 6d (2½p) per annum per post, and a larger board on a grass plot in North Parade for directing visitors to the lower terminus, on payment of 1s (5p) per annum. The company had by now been successful in its search for a general manager, Mr George White having been 'poached' from the Liverpool Overhead Railway. The first secretary to the company, Mr A. G. Pugh, had already been appointed.

INSPECTIONS AND OPENINGS

On Wednesday 30 July the tramway was visited by Colonel von Donop, representing the Board of Trade, who, according to the *North Wales Chronicle* of 9 August:

> made a careful inspection of the work accomplished. He put the system, known as the tail-rope, to a severe test, letting the cars down rapidly and putting on the brakes quickly, and in many ways testing the soundness of the system and its working. He expressed himself generally satisfied, and intimated that everything was efficient with the exception of one or two minor details.

Although Sir George Newnes, promotor of the Matlock cable tramway and the Lynton & Lynmouth cliff railway, had been chosen as second choice to the Prince of Wales to open the line, the directors decided that any revenue lost in the process was too important to be wasted. The lower section of the tramway therefore opened without delay on the day following Col von Donop's visit, Thursday, 31 July 1902. Hurried arrangements were made in the morning and, as the first car moved out of the lower terminus in the afternoon, the cheers of the onlookers mingled with the strain of 'God Save the King' from the assembled instruments of the town band. When the line closed a few hours later 439 passengers had been carried.

Page 71: The GOR 1974: *(above)* Victoria Station from Church Walks; *(below)* Victoria Station from Old Road. The original terminus was in the yard off to the right.

Since the weekend following the opening was August Bank Holiday weekend the tramway was all set for a favourable start to life and, thanks to some excellent weather for most of the week, this was achieved. During the holiday weekend over 5,000 passengers were carried – 3,000 being on the Monday alone. The *Chronicle* of 9 August remarked that it was:

> a sufficient number to indicate that a great success is awaiting this enterprising venture when it is complete. The difficulty on Monday was that the tram did not run frequently enough and kept people waiting at the stations, but this will surely be altered when the line gets into complete working order. Many persons went up the Orme on the tramway, who had never before been on it, although they had stayed in Llandudno for years.

The service was operated at 15 minute intervals and by the end of the first complete week nearly 12,000 single journeys had been made. By 8 October, the virtual end of the holiday season, the figure had risen to 70,000. At the end of the year the line closed for overhaul, having carried 75,738 passengers and collected a total revenue of £925 3s 10d (£925.19) of which no less than £922 17s 3d (£922.86) came from passenger receipts. Against this was set an expenditure of £527 13s 3d (£527.66) and the sum of £397 10s 7d (£397.53) was forwarded to the next half-year's accounts. These figures were reported with evident satisfaction at the GOT Co's half-yearly meeting on 6 March 1903. J. L. Mayger and T. Esmor Hooson (who had joined the board since the incorporation of the company) were re-elected as directors.

It was hoped to reopen the lower section of the tramway (it had closed after Saturday 3 January) at Easter after the work of overhauling, repairing and checking the line had been carried out; the work was progressing satisfactorily. As regards the upper section though, the outlook was not quite so bright. To oversee the construction work Mr G. C. Aitchison, secretary and general manager of the Snowdon Mountain Tramroad and described by the *Chronicle* of 14 March 1903 as 'an expert in mountain railways', was appointed as a consulting engineer. The result was, according to the same report, that 'the work on the upper portion of the tramway is progressing satisfactorily under his supervision'. The chairman of the board reported that 'owing to unforeseen difficulties the upper section of tramroad had not yet been inspected by the Board of Trade, but arrangements were in hand for opening the line to the summit as early as possible'. Conway also reported with satisfaction that during the last half-year another 514 shares had been allotted and a further allotment would take place early that month.

The date originally planned for the opening of the upper section was Whitsun but, while the lower section opened as intended on Easter Monday, this was not to be. The newly-completed portion was inspected by Col von Donop on 8 May; the following extract from the *Chronicle* of 30 May describes the event:

> Colonel von Donop, on behalf of the Board of Trade, recently inspected the upper section of the Great Orme's Head Tramroad, and, subject to certain minor alterations, the Board of Trade have passed the line and the cars for traffic. As soon as the changes required, which are chiefly connected with the brakes to the cars, have been carried out the railway will be worked to the summit. In the meantime the cars are running every quarter of an hour on the lower section up to the plateau.

After the necessary modifications had been made the upper portion was again inspected on 7 July and passed for traffic. The opening took place the next morning, Wednesday, without ceremony. The tramway was at last fully operational.

DEVELOPMENTS, DISPUTES – AND DANGER

For three years the GOT was surrounded by a flurry of activity which then abruptly died down, leaving the tramway to operate without major incident for a long period. The main developments centred on the two termini of the tramway; at the lower a new station was planned and at the upper a hotel and golf course. Early in 1903 Llandudno UDC had approached the GOT Co with regard to the state of the footpath in front of the station in Church Walks. The tramway company replied that it was willing 'to curb and channel' the path when the site had been developed in the near future. As the footpath had in fact never been kerbed or guttered before this answer was accepted.

The number of passengers carried in 1903 was 77,410, slightly down on the previous year. To the profit earned was added another £1,000 in an increased share issue to pay for the construction of a new lower terminus. This task occupied the winter of 1903–4 and involved demolishing the Victoria Hotel building and removing the curve into the old hotel yard terminus, the line now carrying straight on parallel with Old Road to the edge of Church Walks. (The hotel had been one of the first to be constructed in Llandudno and was for a long time the principal hotel there.) At the same time three stone carsheds were erected: one at the upper end of the lower section and one at each end of the upper section. Each held one car, the fourth passenger car being housed in the new station, known as Victoria Station.

Meanwhile work was progressing at the summit on the development of the whole of the area. The 1898 Act empowered the company to build a hotel there but as it found difficulty in even raising sufficient capital to build the tramway it offered the chance of constructing the hotel elsewhere. The *North Wales Chronicle* of 7 February 1903 announced that Mr Griffith B. Morgan, the catering manager of the Great Northern Railway and the owner of the Clarence Hotel in Llandudno, had recently purchased the 'Old Telegraph Inn' at the summit and proposed to spend £2,000 on extending the building to make it suitable for the increased business the tramway was expected to bring. Three weeks later Morgan was advertising for tenders for the construction of refreshment rooms adjacent to the Telegraph Inn. By the end of May the old buildings had been virtually demolished and an application granted to Morgan to erect a marquee for the summer trade, presumably a temporary measure while the hotel was completed. On 4 September the first ascent of the Great Orme by a motor car was made.

The contract for building the new hotel was awarded to Thomas McDonald, of Dundalk, who began work in April 1903. By 1904 however, with the hotel only half completed, Morgan (who had been made a GOT Co director) went bankrupt; the one-storey structure was taken over by the Liverpool Docks Trustees to track ships bound for the Mersey. Morgan's other interest at the summit, a 175 acre golf course under construction on land leased from the Mostyn estate, was acquired by local golfers who formed a club for the purpose.

The last major alteration to take place concerned the crossing of Tygwyn Road by the tramway. As originally laid the crossing was widely regarded as unsafe and gave the UDC especially much cause for concern. As early as September 1902 the tramway company had agreed to pay the council the sum of £17 10s (£17.50) towards the cost of putting Tygwyn Road in repair; there was also a dispute over the residents' path from Black Gate up the road. (Black Gate, or Iron Gate, was where Old Road joined Tygwyn Road.) The matter appears to have rested there until November 1903 when the council informed the GOT Co that unless the unsafe condition of the road was rectified the Board of Trade would have to be informed. In March of the following year the town surveyor met the tramway directors to discuss the situation and the company agreed, after the coming season, to take up all the track there and relay it on a more southerly site which meant crossing Tygwyn Road at more of a right angle. They also undertook to take up the existing setts and relay them and the rails more carefully to provide wooden in lieu of iron covers for pulley pits, and to make the gate to open further back. Thus can be deduced the essential points of disagreement! This arrangement was to the satisfaction of the UDC though complaints were naturally still made throughout the year. In August the council requested that the company place a man at the crossing while the trams were running until the end of the season, because of the continued danger but it is not known whether this action was actually carried out. The matter did not end there for the start of the work on the track alteration was continually held up by lack of money. The proposed new layout was not inspected by von Donop until 19 June 1906; he approved the plans and the work was at last executed the following winter.

One last dispute during this period deserves mention. This was a civil action arising from the construction of the tramway. The plaintiffs, T. & J. Owen, issued a writ for £80 19s 2d (£80.96) which they claimed was owing to them from the defendants, R. White & Sons. The plaintiffs had been employed by the defendants to perform certain preliminary work on the tramway construction and later undertook some sub-contracting for them. The work had been completed by 1 August 1901 but the balance outstanding for the work had not been paid. The defendants had promised to do this on receipt of a certificate for the work from their engineer, Enfield Taylor, but this had not been forthcoming. The plaintiffs denied that their work had been in any way defective and instigated legal proceedings. The case was heard at Chester County Court at the end of July 1903 before Sir Horatio Lloyd then adjourned until November. The defendants then claimed that £500 had been paid in respect of a total bill of £580 19s 2d (£580.96) but the work in question, a concrete conduit, had not been completed and the defendants had had to finish it themselves. The case was then adjourned until the following March when, after three days of investigation and decision making, the judge awarded the plaintiffs damages of £67 12s (£67.60).

There then followed a long, relatively uneventful era of operations though during the 1900s several seasons were far from satisfactory financially – sometimes the line only worked a six week season. In 1906 White was succeeded as manager by Mr Henry Sutcliffe; in 1909 and 1911 two minor collisions took place but without serious damage or injury; in 1918 the tramway only operated for a total of twenty-two days as a new cable was needed and a permit could not be obtained from the Ministry of Munitions because of the war effort. Underneath this apparent calm, though, several disturbing factors were quietly at work, awaiting only for the chance and right circumstances to align themselves in a disastrous – and tragic – combination.

Page 77: The GOR 1974: *(above)* No 4 descending at the Tyn y Coed Road/Tygwyn Road corner. The gradient is not exaggerated by the camera; *(below)* No 5 squeezing through Old Road. Note the coupler – a remnant of the jockey car days.

MISFORTUNE STRIKES

On Sunday 21 August 1932 the drawbar of one of the lower section cars (No 5) snapped in two, though luckily the car had been halted without any mishap. Just two days later the same thing happened, this time with far more terrible consequences:

> All Llandudno was horrified on Tuesday to learn that one of the cable cars of the Great Orme tramway had run away, crushing to death the driver, Edward Harris, and creating some shocking injuries among the crowd of visitors who, a moment before, had been gaily singing as they returned from a happy morning on the summit of the Orme. A little girl, Margaret Worthington, whose foot was torn off, died at 3pm in the hospital.
>
> (*North Wales Chronicle* 26 August 1932)

The accident occurred shortly after noon on Tabor Hill, just above Black Gate. As the *Chronicle* continued:

> Careering for a short distance at gathering speed, the tram left the metals and crashed into a twelve foot high wall. A tramway standard caught in its flight was torn up, a portion being flung into a neighbouring lane. As the top of the tram swept along the crest of the wall, it dislodged the coping stones which cascaded through the window spaces upon the passengers. The car was full of people, there probably being thirty-five persons on it.

At the moment of collision the car's occupants were hurled violently forward, many breaking their heads on the window frames. The wall in question was that on the left (looking downhill) at the top of the narrow Old Road. The unfortunate brakeman on the front platform tried to jump to safety but tragically chose the wrong side for the car lurched over, crushing him against the wall. Riding on the platform with him was twelve-year-old Margaret Worthington who had been to take her father, an employee of the tramway company, his lunch at the summit. Harris had courageously grabbed the young girl and leapt from the tram with her in his arms. There she was found, alive but badly injured, pinned by the weight of the car against the wall. She could not be freed until help arrived to move the tram but by then it was too late; she died three hours later in hospital. The conductor, Jim Coleburn, who had been riding on the rear platform, had also jumped and had escaped uninjured.

The scene was one of utter chaos with crowds of onlookers and heroic rescue workers, many of whom were themselves injured passengers, and a constant ambulance shuttle service taking the casualties to hospital. In all two died, eleven were kept in the hospital for treatment and three others treated there for cuts and shock. One of those badly injured was the wife of Rabbi Levin of Manchester – who escaped unscathed, as did the Bishop of Killaloe, another passenger. With the injured removed the area was roped-off and the car, No 4, secured by ropes to two convenient trees to await the Ministry of Transport investigation.

The inquiry, held by Lt Col E. P. Anderson, took place the following Monday in the town hall. It lasted one hour; the scene of the accident had previously been inspected by Anderson. In the words of the *Chronicle* of 2 September, 'Several facts of interest were disclosed during the course of the inquiry'. One was when the manager, Sutcliffe, recounted how a drawbar had broken the Sunday before the accident. It had been, he said, a unique occurrence. All the drawbars were identical, made of 'Vibrac' steel, and had been supplied by Craven Bros Ltd of Manchester. A representative of this company said that the drawbars were capable of taking a direct strain of 3–400 tons; he was of the opinion that 'the break had occurred sideways and not in the direction of the tension'. Sutcliffe stated that the company – the GOT Co – 'did not specify any particular strength or analysis. The makers knew the conditions. There was no specifications with the drawbars previously supplied.'

At Anderson's insistence the broken drawbar was produced by the police. It had been manufactured to a uniform thickness of $\frac{3}{4}$in to enable it to run in the conduit slot, which was $1\frac{1}{4}$in wide, allowing room for clearance. On being measured it was discovered that the drawbar had been worn down $\frac{1}{8}$in in thickness – by what Sutcliffe termed 'surface rubbing' – since its fitting *on 15 August*. The next intriguing piece of information was remarkable by its absence: though the car's wheel and slipper brakes (see Chapter 6) were both found to be hard on, they had failed to halt the runaway progress of the car (243ft along the rails after parting company with the cable and a further 75ft down the roadway). Of the emergency slot brake, which should have been sufficient to stop the car, *there was no mention*. The rest of the investigation was conducted in private.

The mystery of the missing emergency brake was cleared up by the publication of the inspecting officer's report on 2 February 1933. It transpired that during the period 1902–6 jerky handling of the winding controls had caused momentary slackness in the cable sufficient to cause the automatic brake to come into play. This brake consisted of two jaws bearing on the Z rails of the conduit slot; the normal tension on the cable held them off. If however the tension was removed, ie by the cable breaking or suddenly slackening, powerful springs forced the jaws against the sides of the conduit. Moreover, the weight of the car continuing downhill was transmitted by means of cams to the jaws, causing them to bear with increasing pressure until the car halted. It was an apparently foolproof and very effective emergency brake; however, the constant interruptions of traffic in the early years (it took several hours' work to release and reset the brake) had resulted in the removal of the brake apparatus and the governor on the winding engine. More important though these actions were apparently taken without the knowledge, let alone approval, of the board of directors.

Lt Col Anderson did not have far to look for the cause of the accident. Besides the disconnection of the emergency brake, he also condemmed the use of steel treated in a way unsuitable for the purpose intended on the tramway, ie the drawbars. He strongly recommended that all similar drawbars should be replaced and that passengers should be prohibited from riding on the front platform. Above all, he emphasised the necessity of complying with statutory regulations. Operations had of course been suspended ever since the accident, pending the publication of the report.

On Monday 13 February the GOT Co held its annual general meeting at which an advisory committee was set up, consisting of three directors and three shareholders, to implement the advice of Anderson's report. Action had already been taken in one direction, for the directors had consulted the Liverpool firm of Messrs Sloan & Lloyd Barnes over the question of a new, trouble-free design of emergency brake. Actual details of this brake were now before the Ministry of Transport for approval. Receipts for 1932 were given as £3,446 10s 11d (£3,446.54½), the overall result being a loss of £91 15s 2d (£91.76) attributable to the suspension of services and the sum of £150 expended on the repairs to car No 4 and the track. The hope was expressed of reopening the line in time for Easter. Mention was made of the fact that in the previous 30 years over four million passengers had been carried without a single accident; the whole tone of the meeting dwelt upon past success rather than present uncertainty. And there was great uncertainty for the directors reluctantly admitted that the company possessed *no* reserve fund and that the claims for compensation (still being finalised) were *not* fully covered by insurance.

The logical outcome of this state of affairs was obvious:

> Surprise was caused in Llandudno yesterday when it became known that a Sheriff's Officer had under a writ of fi. fa., taken possession of the Great Orme Tramway Co. The first intimation of this unexpected development that the townspeople had was the appearance of bills announcing that the county bailiff, Mr. W. Owen, F.I.A., of Llandudno, would "sell by public auction at the Victoria Station, Church Walks, on Monday, June 12th, the whole of the fixtures, fittings, and office equipment, relating to the Great Orme Tramway Company, and including 4½ miles of tram rails, approximately 870 yards of steel cable, and four tram cars (48 seats)."
>
> (*North Wales Weekly News* 8 June 1933)

This action came three weeks after a suit for damages by Rabbi Harris Levin and his wife Sarah of Cheetham Hill, Manchester, for £4,000 damages in respect of injuries and shock received in the accident. The suit was settled for £1,000 plus costs. Thus the company failed in its attempt to persuade those claiming against the tramway to wait until the line was working again and thus earning revenue out of which they could be paid. The company's financial position can best be judged by the fact that it was unable to meet even Levin's reduced claim and therefore applied for and obtained a writ of *fi. fa.* (a sheriff's order to sell the goods of a debtor in execution of a judgement).

An emergency meeting of the GOT Co was held on 7 June under the chairmanship of alderman John Owen. They had little choice in the circumstances but to file a petition in the High Court for a compulsory winding-up order. Mr R. Vincent Johnson, director and solicitor for the GOT Co, spoke of being fair to the other creditors. (Other claims lodged against the company amounted to a further £10,000.) He stated that there was 'no reason why the trams should not be operated after the liquidation, because an asset to the town as valuable as this could not be allowed to disappear'. They were prophetic words.

THE GREAT ORME RAILWAY LTD

Matters were meanwhile well in hand to get the tramway running again. A new set of emergency brakes had been ordered from Walker Bros of Wigan (see Chapter 6 for details) and one had been fitted to car No 5 and tested in April 1933. Testing continued throughout the summer while the winding-up petition was adjourned for a month to see if some agreement could be reached with the company's creditors. No such agreement was forthcoming though and on Monday 24 July, in the Chancery Division, Mr Justice Bennett made an order for the compulsory liquidation of the Great Orme Tramway Co. The petition was not opposed.

A creditors' meeting was held on 25 August and it was decided that their best hope was to continue the brake tests with a view of reopening the line and then selling it as a going concern.

Page 83: The GOR 1974: *(above)* in the cutting below Summit Station; *(below)* No 4 awaits the upper section connection at Halfway.

A public test of the brake on No 5, laden with scrap iron, was held on 23 March 1934 before cine cameras. It was a success and Walker Bros subsequently equipped No 4 in a similar fashion. Successful too was the Ministry of Transport's inspection (by Col A. C. Trench) on 11 May of that year and less than a week later, on Thursday 17 May, the tramway reopened. A new regulation imposed as an aftermath of the 1932 accident was a compulsory brake test each spring before the seasonal opening. Also successful was the summer operation and the line was accordingly offered for sale.

In December 1934 the tramway was sold for £5,600 to a syndicate which originated from the shareholders' committee and the new owners set about forming a limited company to operate the line in 1935. Thus on 25 March 1935 the Great Orme Railway Ltd was registered with a capital of £10,000 in £1 shares. The six directors were John E. Anstiss (draper), Hugh Edwards (painter), Arthur Hewitt (architect), Sir William M. Letts, John E. Payne (cafe proprietor) and Arthur Sutcliffe (described as a gentleman). All were local men.

The line opened for the summer season in 1935 and continued to do business as usual; operation was not interrupted by World War II though the summit hotel building was converted into an RAF radar station. After the war the hotel was bought by Randolph Turpin, the boxer, but the project failed and it was acquired by the council which leased it to the Forte organisation.

Apart from slight changes in identification resulting from the new name, and several service changes (see Chapter 6), the only major event which happened during the tramway's period of new ownership was when, at the end of the 1945 season, the manager, Henry Sutcliffe, was succeeded by Mr C. C. Rhodes. His retirement in effect marked the end of the old order for just two years later Llandudno UDC decided to buy the tramway.

UNDER CIVIC OWNERSHIP

In the provisions of the 1898 authorising Act the Llandudno Urban District Council had been given the option of buying the

Great Orme tramway after a period of 28 years had elapsed (ie in 1926) or at seven yearly intervals thereafter. When one such opportunity came round in 1947 the council took the decision to exercise this option and served the necessary notice on the GOR Ltd. (The council had actually been offered the tramway in 1910 and had then offered £7,000 for it. The shareholders however had refused to ratify the directors' proposal to sell it at that price.) The tramway company calculated that the price the council would have to pay would be £26,000 – a figure based on capital expended since 1898 (£19,464) plus interest. The council took exception to this unrealistic figure in view of the fact that the line had been purchased in 1935 for only £5,600 to which could be added further capital expenditure of £1,370. The council was supported in this view by Mr Justice Jenkins in the High Court's Chancery Division when he ruled that the purchase price was to be based on outlay since 1935 only which, plus interest, gave a compulsory purchase price of £8,407. The payment was made by the council on 24 November 1948, backdated to 31 March, and civic ownership took effect as from New Year's Day. The GOR Ltd was then left with little else to do but wind itself up voluntarily with its last meeting on 25 March 1950. Final settlement to the shareholders amounted to 33s 9d (£1.69) per £1 share.

After some track relaying had been carried out on the lower section the tramway opened again at Easter as usual and continued to prosper, though in the following year (1950) the council introduced competition for the line in the shape of a bus service from the town hall to St Tudno's church. This service also ran in the winter months as far as Tyn y Coed and has proved a boon to residents living on the Orme. Further track renewal was later carried out, made possible by good returns from the line (some ¼ million passengers were being carried annually), but by the mid-1950s it became clear that costs were rising far too rapidly and some method of reducing them would have to be found. The most obvious area in which economies could be made was that of power. The boiler house at Halfway burnt 250 tons of coke each year at a cost of £7 per ton. It was estimated that if the winding house was converted to electricity

Page 86: The GOR 1974: *(above)* Summit Station with car No 6; in the distance is Anglesey; *(below)* the upper section passing loop. Note point lever and car indicators in the cage, Halfway Station in centre, GOC pylons on left, Llandudno in distance.

then some £1,400 could be saved each year; thus in 1956 a contract was placed with the English Electric Co for the necessary equipment and the steam engines were used for the last time during the 1957 season. By the time the tramway reopened in 1958 the conversion had been carried out. (See Chapter 6 for details of the equipment.)

Since then little change has been made to either the tramway or its working, though in 1965 a brick passenger shelter was erected at the Summit Station. At the beginning of August 1966 a slight mishap occurred on the upper section when the rear bogie of a Summit-bound car took the wrong line at the passing loop, causing the two cars to collide. No-one was hurt in the incident but the tramway was out of action for several days while the damage was repaired. In 1968 Mr Rhodes, the general manager, retired at the end of the season and was succeeded by Mr Eric Woodyeat, the manager of the UDC motor buses, who took the position of transport manager for the council, covering both systems. In the following year a second rival appeared on the scene in the form of the Great Orme Cabinlift; further details of this installation are given in Chapter 9.

Monday 30 July 1972 the 70th anniversary of the Great Orme Tramway was celebrated (albeit one day early) with cheering crowds, Edwardian costumes and the 11.00am car conducted by the chairman of the council, Mr Harold Gott. Also present was Mr E. Johnson, representative of Messrs R. White & Sons, suppliers of the original track and winding gear. Every passenger that day was presented with a special commemorative certificate to mark the occasion; special one-day covers were also sold. In 1973 the line joined, for marketing purposes, the growing ranks of the 'Great Little Trains of Wales', a fitting way to honour the principality's last surviving tramway. Following the reorganisation of local government the tramway, as from 1 April 1974, is now under the control of Aberconwy District Council – which body absorbed the former Llandudno UDC.

The 75th anniversary of the line was celebrated over the weekend of 30–31 July 1977. The scenes were much as for the 70th anniversary with decorated cars, travellers in period costume and so forth. On the Sunday over 2,000 people were carried and at Victoria Station the Mayor of Aberconwy, Councillor K. David Jones, unveiled a plaque commemorating the tramway's history.

The working of the GOT is fully explained in the next chapter but it is perhaps appropriate to mention here that although passenger figures fell slightly in 1976 compared with 1975 (191,490 and 208,000 respectively), the high standard of current maintenance augurs well for its long-term survival. In 1976 for example, a new type of oil-impregnated nylon bush was tested on a cable pulley on the lower section with satisfactory results and a further twenty-five ordered for the 1977 season. If the longer trials prove equally successful then the whole of the lower section will be so treated. The advantages of the new bushes are that they need no lubrication, less inspection and are easily replaced. A boon to local lineside residents is that they are also quieter! Before the 1978 season some £28,000 was spent on repairs to the track – also on the lower section – and further expenditure is planned. One result was that the line did not operate an Easter service that year – certainly the first time it had failed to do so for a great many years.

6 Up the Orme

THE FUNICULAR SYSTEM

The Great Orme tramway is unique in the British Isles and the specialised function of much of its equipment, the purely mechanical side of the tramway, deserves close inspection. This facet of the line can best be divided into three sections – permanent way, the winding gear, and the telegraphic link between the cars and the winding house.

The permanent way

The rails used on both 3ft 6in gauge sections are 50lb/yd flat bottom type, manufactured in Workington and supplied by White & Sons together with points and crossings (manufactured in Sheffield by Askham Bros & Wilson Ltd). On the upper section the rails are bolted to wooden sleepers, lightly ballasted, laid on the ground. On the lower section an entirely different arrangement was called for. Here the rails are bolted to short sleepers laid in a bed of concrete and connected by ties to two parallel Z section girders laid down the centre of the track. The girders form a 6in wide conduit, 14in deep with a 1¼in gap between the girder flanges at the top; the haulage cable runs within the conduit. The running rails are fitted with continuous guard rails (a specification of the Board of Trade – the GOT Co had intended to use grooved tramway rails) and the whole is paved flush with the rail and conduit surfaces. On the roadway stretch this is done with tarmac and on the reserved roadside stretch up to Halfway with concrete.

On the lower section the cable runs in the conduit supported on grooved sheaves and guided round curves by vertical pulleys spaced at 6ft intervals. The pulleys are mounted in a special housing with an access cover in the roadway for lubrication and maintenance purposes. On the upper section the cable runs exposed (except for short road crossings) on similar sheaves and

Page 90: GOR trackwork: *(above left)* the lower section passing loop (bottom end); *(above right)* the lower section passing loop (showing interlaced track at top end); *(below)* cable guide mechanisms on the upper section.

pulleys. At the upper section passing loop the two points are worked by the passage of the cars with each car setting the points as it trails through the switch blades ready for its return along the same path. Hand levers are also fitted but they are locked inside wire cages to prevent any possible tampering. On the top of each lever (one on each side of the running line) is a circular indicator bearing a number corresponding to the number of the car using that side of the loop. The fact that each car sets the points behind it when it leaves means that it always takes the same track through the loop (ie north or south track), as indeed it must do to prevent the cables from crossing. Guarded breaks in the running rails allow passage of the cable. It is unusual with this type of operation to have worked switches with moving blades. On such lines abroad, particularly in Switzerland, points have fixed rails with gaps but the cars have double flanged wheels on one side and unflanged wheels on the other. The two cars have their flanged wheels on opposite sides to guide them consistently along the same side of the loops. Double flanged wheels could not be used with the flush road surface of the Great Orme line.

A similar worked set of points controls entry to and exit from the lower end of the loop on the lower section with a wide junction slot where the conduit divides. (At night and during the winter this is protected by a metal cover.) At the upper end of the loop the two tracks merely converge to become – just within the definition – interlaced, the two nearest rails running together to form a common running rail/guard rail unit. This arrangement provides a 'single line' while at the same time allows two separate conduits to be used, each in the centre of their own track, so that the ascending and descending cables do not meet on the sharp curves and therefore foul the pulleys – as would happen if a common conduit was used. This problem is avoided on the upper section by the fact that off-centre drawbars are used on the cars, enabling the separate cables to run between one pair of rails with sufficient distance between them to prevent fouling.

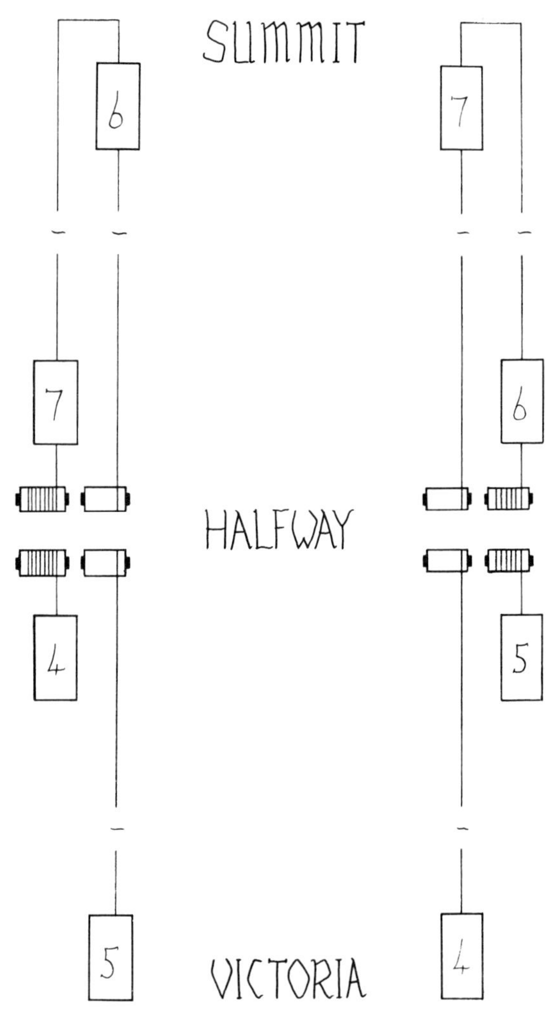

9 Great Orme Tramway winding diagram showing the two extremes of travel

The winding gear

As installed for the opening of the line, this was a steam-powered plant comprising one boiler and two colliery-type winding engines. The locomotive-type boiler (with a second, smaller one in reserve) was built by Roby of Lincoln. It supplied steam at just over 100lb/sq in pressure to the two engines, one for each section. Both the latter were originally supplied by C. & A. Musker of Liverpool, that working the lower section having an output of 80hp and that of the upper section 60hp. The former engine later replaced the latter and a new 120hp engine was purchased from the Sandicroft Foundry, Chester, for the lower section. All three engines were of a two-cylinder design and were governor controlled to a constant speed. Each of the pair in use drove a shaft fitted with two winding drums, one wound the opposite way to the other so that on turning one would wind cable in while the other let it out, and vice versa, thus working the two cars on each section of the tramway.

During the winter of 1957/8 the original plant was removed and replaced by completely new gear installed by the English Electric Co. Each drum shaft is now driven by a 50Hz 3 phase slip ring induction motor, supplied with electricity at 415V. That working the lower section shaft is rated at 125hp and that of the upper at 75hp. Both run at 730rpm and are geared down to give drum speeds of 25rpm and 35rpm for the lower and upper sections respectively. To ensure smooth starting and stopping a drum controller operating rotor resistances controls the motor speeds. These controls are mounted on a common control panel, together with an emergency stop switch and handbrake wheel. The last mentioned operates by screw-down brakes on the winding drums. A weight-operated brake is also incorporated in the equipment and is continually held in the 'off' position whenever the current is on by an electro-hydraulic thruster; if the emergency stop button is pushed, or a centrifugal trip on one of the motors (set to cut-out at 15 per cent overspeed) comes into action, then so does the emergency brake. The screw handbrake provides the normal means of control braking and is fully interlocked with the rest of the controls. The two sets of controls are the separate responsibility of two engineers, one for each section.

A week before Easter every year the equipment is checked by the Department of Transport (formerly the Ministry of Transport) and the gear drive modified, by temporary belts, to produce a drum speed high enough to cause the cars on the lower section to pass their pre-set brake limits and so test their emergency brakes.

As is to be expected, since the winding house is only halfway up the line of the tramway and not at the summit, different methods of moving the cars have to be employed on the two sections. On the lower section this is simply done by using two separate steel cables, each $1\frac{5}{16}$ in in diameter, $\frac{1}{2}$ mile long and with a breaking strain of 60 tons. One is wound onto each drum and attached to one car; consequently when one is wound up the other is lowered down and vice versa. On the upper section three separate cables are used, each with a diameter of $\frac{7}{8}$in and a breaking strain of 30 tons. One is wound onto one drum and linked to one car; the second is attached to the other end of that car and continues to the summit, round an idler there and back down to join the second car. The third cable runs from the other end of *that* car down to the other drum in the winding house. Thus, when the drum shaft is rotated in the appropriate direction, the car at the summit is pulled *down* to Halfway Station, pulling *up* the other car in the process. As the ascending car is also connected by cable to the winding house the braking of one automatically produces the same effect upon the other regardless of which way it is travelling.

The telegraph system

As the tramway is operated as a remotely controlled funicular railway, a system of communication between the conductor in the car and the controller in the winding house is of paramount importance. The system adopted when the tramway was constructed is still in use today and consists of a bell and telephone link between both cars on one section and their controller in the winding house. Hand-generators in the car supply the necessary current for the telephones and bells. Communication is effected by the overhead wire to which the cars are connected by trolleys (see below). The wire is carried along the route by roadside standards and supporting brackets in a similar manner to an overhead current supply for a more conventional tramway – indeed it is sometimes mistaken for exactly that though the equipment is much lighter than would otherwise be the case. Both loops have two overhead wires to allow the two cars' trolleys to pass, though the second wire was not added to the upper section loop until 1949. Before that date the conductor of the descending car would lower his trolley from the wire while the other car passed.

MAKING THE ASCENT

A typical journey on the Great Orme tramway, for an observant passenger, goes somewhat in this fashion. A ticket is purchased at the booking office window at Victoria Station. This window is set in the side of the one-storey building which houses the manager's office and which forms one side of the station premises. From this building projects an overall roof to protect the 'platform' area and the one terminal road. The other three sides of the premises are open (though railed-off) with Church Walks at the bottom and Old Road to the side opposite the office block. Car No 4 or 5 is boarded when it arrives (if it is not already waiting), from ground level, there being no platforms in the conventional sense anywhere along the tramway. On leaving the terminus the car moves out into Old Road past the site of the original terminus on the left in the former Victoria Hotel yard, 90ft above sea level.

The line climbs up the centre of the narrow roadway with its stone walls on each side. As there is no room whatsoever for another vehicle to squeeze past, other traffic is prohibited from using the roadway during the hours of tramway operation. The gradient over this stretch fluctuates between 1 in 4.4 and 1 in 3.6 – the steepest portion is at the top of Old Road where the line enters and crosses Tygwyn Road at Black Gate. This is the first request stop on the tramway and the scene of the fatal 1932 accident; a large convex mirror on one side of the line enables the driver of a descending car to see any traffic about to come round the blind corner at the junction. Continuing up the right-hand side of Tygwyn Road, the line occupies its own unfenced reservation, slightly above the level of the road surface. Almost immediately the passing loop is reached and the descending car passed. The loop is positioned a little below the actual halfway mark on the section.

Above the loop the two tracks converge to form the interlaced track described in the previous section. This continues all the way up to Halfway Station. A short distance past the loop comes Tyn y Coed Road junction on the left and the tramway's second and final request stop. The line steepens its climb and swings round to the right, still paralleling the road, and then to the left. It now leaves the road which veers leftwards once more and both tramway and road enter the open heathland of the Great Orme plateau. Here the ascending car comes gently to rest outside its stone shed, beyond which stands the winding house and beyond that the car shed for that end of the upper section. Here the passengers alight, following the instruction of a large notice which reads

CHANGE HERE FOR SUMMIT-CAR

This is the logically named Halfway Station, originally (and equally logically) known as the First Station. At 489ft above sea level the station is exactly 400ft above the lower terminus and 872 track yards from it. The average gradient climbed in that distance is 1 in 6.5.

Passing round the stone-built winding house and car sheds the passengers await the arrival of car No 6 or 7 from the summit. The difference in the trackwork of the two sections is immediately apparent; not so apparent but still faintly traceable are the remains of the linking track between the two sections and the siding to serve the boiler house. The journey over the upper section commences on the level then begins to rise along a low embankment to the site of the passing loop. Though on a private right of way the track is unfenced – in spite of the early wishes of Lord Mostyn – and, in the true British tradition for all minor lines wandering through open countryside, sheep and cattle are a constant hazard. Leaving the loop behind the embankment gives way to a short cutting where the gradient stiffens to 1 in 10.3, the steepest on this section. Then Summit Station is reached, 827yd from Halfway and just out of sight from it. The station consists of a stone car shed similar to those at Halfway (the car again stops just short of it) and the brick shelter erected in 1965. At 650ft above sea level it is just 29ft below the actual summit of the Orme and 161ft above Halfway. The average gradient over the upper section is 1 in 15.5.

The view from the summit of the Great Orme is the reason for the very existence of the tramway and it is without doubt truly impressive. From a vantage point seemingly poised midway between land and sea, the coastline extends far on each side, especially majestic in appearance to the west with its jutting headlands; behind the coastal development and settlement and across the broad estuary and valley of the Conway rise the mountains of Snowdonia; before lies the Irish Sea stretching out to the horizon, broken only by the backbone of the Isle of Man and, on exceptionally clear days, by the mountains of the Lake District in England and the Wicklow Hills in Ireland.

OPERATION

The actual running of the cars on either section is controlled by the engineer in the winding house and the driver on each car. Communication between them is effected by way of the telephone and bell apparatus mentioned above. On the lower section the apparatus is used in this manner: before starting from Victoria Station the driver gives a signal, by means of the bell-push on the roof above him, to the bell on the engineer's control board. Two short rings means that he is ready to start and has no need to stop en route; one long and one short means that he is ready to start and requires to stop at Black Gate; one short and one long means he is ready to start and requires to stop at Tyn y Coed Road; two long rings means stop at both halts. (The engineer needs this information to be able to halt the cars where the ascending driver wishes to stop; he does this by judging the amount of cable wound up.) The driver of the descending car does not normally give any signals but informs his opposite number when he is ready to start. If the ascending car stops, then of course so does he. An emergency stop by either driver is achieved by one ring on the bell; restarting is by two.

By releasing the brake on the winding drums the engineer sets the two cars in motion at a constant speed (5mph) and by applying the screw brake he stops the cars where needed and at the end of the journey. The drivers on the cars do not use their own brakes for normal running.

Page 98: GOR – Halfway Station: *(above)* the sign; *(below)* the lower section car shed with former connection relic; 1974.

A somewhat similar arrangement is in force on the upper section, with the communication between drivers and the signal to start from the lower one. There are no request stops to signal. Both drivers operate their handbrakes during the journey for the constant cable speed is 7mph and the more varied gradient necessitates the cable being kept taut all the time so as not to foul the pulleys. (If an emergency stop is made the cable has to be checked before restarting to ensure that no fouling has occurred.) At night both cars on the upper section run slightly further than they are permitted to do during the day and enter their respective car sheds, one at the summit and one at Halfway. On the lower section, with one car in Victoria Station the other is outside its shed at Halfway and at night has to be eased in by pulling the descending cable out of its conduit in a loop.

Besides the two engineers and four drivers, the rest of the staff consists of four conductors (who issue tickets where necessary), two maintenance men, the booking clerk at Victoria and the general manager – a total of fourteen, some of whom are employed only seasonally when the line is open.

SERVICES AND FARES

Like most other seasonal pleasure lines, the Great Orme tramway's season extends from Easter through to early October. This has always been the case (with the one exception of 1902 when it stayed open till the end of the year), in spite of the expressed intentions to run a winter service for the benefit of residents along the lower section of the line. As was the UDC's privilege under the 1898 Act, the running of trams on Sundays was forbidden until 1935; the principle of Sabbath observance was strongly held in the town during the early years of the century and the tramway was not alone in feeling the restriction. With the commencement of Sunday running the service was operated in an identical fashion seven days a week.

No hard-and-fast timetable has ever been employed on the tramway for the very nature and shortness of the sections make such regimentation pointless. Instead the line is run to suit the demands of the season, beginning and ending with four cars an hour and, at the holiday peak, eight cars an hour. Similar variation can be introduced for a day's working if the weather or other circumstances render it necessary. Eight cars an hour is the limit for each section, for the journey times are 5½–6 minutes on the lower and 4½–5 on the upper. Hours of operation have varied little over the years, starting between 9.00am and 10.00am and finishing just before dusk (the actual time of course again depending on the time of year).

While the pattern of services shows so little change the pattern of fares has altered considerably – inevitably going up as the years have passed. Under the 1898 Act the permitted charges (not to be varied on Sundays or Bank Holidays) were fixed at 6d (2½p) single and 9d (3½p) return. For shorter journeys the GOT Co could charge as it thought fit – as it also could for invalid carriages or other special accommodation. A passenger's free luggage allowance was 28lb. Goods, minerals and parcels were to be carried but livestock was excluded. The charges for parcels were:

Weight	*Cost*
Up to 7lb	3d (1½p)
Between 7lb and 14lb	5d (2p)
Between 14lb and 28lb	7d (3p)
Between 28lb and 56lb	9d (3½p)

At an early date season tickets were offered for sale to residents and golfers using the summit course. In August 1906, at Lord Mostyn's instigation, additional single fares were introduced for the benefit of residents: these were 1d between Victoria and Black Gate and 2d between Victoria and Halfway, both applicable in either direction. A similar 2d fare was introduced at the same time for the trip over the upper section only.

Under the Statutory Undertakings (Temporary Increase of Charges) Act 1918 and the Tramways (Temporary Increase of Charges) Act 1920 the full single and return fares were raised to 8d (3½p) and 1s (5p) respectively. These continued until 1934 when the new owner, the Great Orme Railway Ltd, discovered that as it was not a statutory company it had no legal power to charge them! The Great Orme Tramway (Temporary Increase of Charges) Order 1934 had therefore to be hurriedly obtained, followed by the Great Orme Tramways Act 1936 solely to authorise the existing fare structure. At this date the cost of season tickets was: weekly, 5s (25p); monthly, 10s 6d (52½p); season, £1. In 1954 the return fare was raised under the Transport Charges (Miscellaneous Provisions) Act to 2s (10p), and again in 1965 to 2s 6d (12½p). After this the fares continued to creep upwards until by 1972 they were:

Ticket	*Cost*
Victoria–Summit (single)	17p
Victoria–Summit (return)	25p
Summit–Victoria (single)	8p
Victoria–Black Gate (resident's)	2p
Victoria–Halfway (resident's)	4p

In all cases children half price.

Up to 1964 the Bell Punch ticket system was used (these are still issued by the conductors) but then strip-tickets were introduced for sale in the booking office. Both sorts are cancelled by the conductors with hand-nippers. Finally, on a slightly macabre note, in the days when the tramway carried corpses to St Tudno's cemetery a charge of 2s 6d (12½p) was made. The mourners paid the usual fare.

ROLLING STOCK

The Great Orme tramway operates with a total fleet of four cars, this being all that is necessary to work the two sections. These are numbered 4–7 and are the survivors of the original fleet of seven. Details of all seven are as follows:

Nos 1–3

The history of these three cars is not as well documented as could be hoped for but enough is known to give a general picture of their construction and use. All were built by Hurst, Nelson & Co of Motherwell, Scotland, and delivered to Llandudno by the LNWR in May 1902. They were not passenger cars at all but were instead intended for carrying freight on the lower section, coke up to the winding house and fuel and other supplies to the hotel at the summit. All three were identical four-wheeled vehicles with an overall length of 16ft 7in. The bodywork consisted of a 9ft long closed centre section and a 2ft 6in open platform at each end. An overall roof was fitted and double folding doors provided in each side. The upper half of the bulkheads were glazed and supplied with doors to allow access through the van. The brakes and drawgear were similar to those on the passenger cars (see below) though an additional brake, a spring-operated snag, was fitted to allow the car to remain at rest unattached. Two of the cars were used for the pre-opening trials over the lower section.

The actual method of working these cars has not unfortunately survived, nor has the history of their eventual disposal. Their quickly-acquired nickname of 'jockey cars' adds weight to the theory that they were propelled up to Halfway by a passenger car and then manhandled either into the boiler house siding or round onto the upper section for pushing up to Summit. P. W. Gentry states that two of the cars were scrapped quite early in the life of the tramway and the third converted to serve as a coke wagon to ferry fuel up to the boiler house before being made redundant by road vehicles. The fact that the passenger cars were equipped with (and still carry) centre couplers and chains suggests that high hopes were once held of using the cars as trailers in a regular fashion. One possibility is that the jockey cars were used to carry coffins up to Summit for burial in St Tudno's churchyard; this is in fact extremely probable since it would have been virtually impossible (and most undignified) to manoeuvre a coffin into one of the passenger cars, lacking the benefit of side doors.

Nos 4–7

These too were built by Hurst, Nelson & Co and were delivered in two lots: Nos 4 and 5 accompanied Nos 1, 2 and 3 and worked the lower section from its opening in 1902 while Nos 6 and 7 arrived in 1903 to open the upper section. The two pairs have worked their respective sections ever since. All are essentially identical with two 4ft wheelbase bogies set at 24ft 4in centres; wheels are 1ft 9in in diameter. On the bogies is mounted the 37ft long body, made up of a 30ft saloon and two open 3ft 6in end platforms. The two bulkheads are glazed and each has a sliding door to allow access to the saloon where the transverse wooden seats provide room for 48 passengers. The seats are arranged back-to-back on each side of the central gangway, abutting onto the roof supports. Above the waistline the vehicles are open and unglazed. A further 12 passengers are permitted to stand. Unladen weight is $6\frac{1}{2}$ tons, laden 10 tons. On the roof are mounted the two trolley poles for the overhead communication wire, one pointing in each direction. The one not in use when ascending or descending is held down by a hook on the roof canopy; formerly this was done by turning the pole back along the roof and tying it down to a cleat on the body below the centre window pillar. The hand-generator, telephone and bell are mounted on the driver's panel on the open end platform – duplicated of course at the other end of the car.

Over the years several minor differences have existed between the cars. No 4, as constructed, was similar to the jockey cars in that it had only one centrally placed trolley pole. It ran in this form for the 1902 season and by 1903 had been equipped with a trolley pole at each end of the roof in a similar manner to Nos 5, 6 and 7. Nos 4 and 5 were originally fitted with curtains to provide some weather protection but they were removed after only two seasons' running – doubtless because of the decision to stop winter services. Oil lamps were also fitted, one at each end, for running at night but this practice was soon abolished. The two lower section cars also carry water tanks, operated by a pedal, for watering the track on curves. As mentioned above, the two upper section cars have off-centre drawgear while on Nos 4 and 5 it is centrally placed.

Brakes

All four cars have – or had – conventional mechanical wheel (shoe) and track (slipper) brakes operated by two brake spindles and wheels mounted outside the dash at each end of the car. (Nos 1, 2 and 3 also appear to have been fitted with these two braking systems.) As constructed, Nos 4 and 5 also had the emergency brake acting on the conduit slot referred to in the previous chapter. This was automatic in its operation: if the cable snapped and the strain on the brake ceased then the weight of the car running downhill caused the brake jaws to be forced with increasing pressure against the sides of the conduit. It was an extremely effective brake and the tragic consequences of its removal have already been shown. In 1934 Nos 4 and 5 were fitted with a new automatic brake in place of the old one. This was supplied by Walker Bros of Wigan and overcame the disadvantages of the earlier one by using instead four skids with steel teeth which come down and dig into the paved surface of the track. The brake is governor-controlled to come into operation at a speed of 25 per cent above the normal, ie at 6¼mph. It is equally effective compared with the old system and can stop a car in half its length. It can also be applied by the driver by another spindle and wheel on either dash. It is in fact now the second driver-controlled brake, for use of the slipper brake would take some of the car's weight off the skid brakes and the slipper brake mechanism has therefore been removed.

Cars No 6 and 7 have only the normal wheel and track brakes. The cable brakes have already been dealt with.

Livery

Originally this was a very attractive deep yellow on the bodywork, with white roofs and white lettering on each side: GREAT ORME TRAMWAYS. The number of the car was repeated before and after the name, again in white. Ironwork and running gear was black. A similar scheme was used for the jockey cars though on these the number was carried on the dashes. At an early date the body colour was changed to unlined royal blue which became progressively darker as the years passed under successive coats of varnish.

In 1962 Nos 4, 5 and 6 were stripped down and repainted bright blue with black lining; No 7 was treated similarly in the following year. Roofs remained white, as did the lettering and numbers while the ironwork and running gear continued to be black. In 1967 all were repainted again, the lighter blue parts reverted to the former royal blue with the addition of cream above the waist – this colour scheme being that later adopted for the UDC's buses. Side lettering from 1934 onwards was GREAT ORME RAILWAY and car numbers were carried on the dashes from then on.

In 1977 the cars were repainted for the 75th anniversary of the line. Lower panels and dashes are in Trafalgar blue while the window frames are ivory, beading is light blue-grey and metal work black. The old-style lettering now reads GREAT ORME TRAMWAY—now once again the tramway's official title.

7 Llandudno & Colwyn Bay Electric Railway

A MATTER OF SOME DOUBT

Of the North Wales tramways, that which linked the two towns of Llandudno and Colwyn Bay had the longest route mileage, the largest car fleet and, at the outset, the greatest problems. Its early history is also by far the most complex, so much so, that many side issues, if set down in detail, would cloud the essentials of the story. In presenting the main and relevant events (and non-events!) I hope that a far clearer account of what took place during this period will result.

The origins of Llandudno have been described in conjunction with the Great Orme Tramway; less than four miles along the coast to the south-east the township of Colwyn Bay experienced a similar boom in the wake of Llandudno's ascension. A century ago the town virtually did not exist; what settlement there was in the area was centred around the villages of (Old) Colwyn, a short distance inland to the east, and Llandrillo yn Rhos, similarly situated to the west. By 1887 it had developed sufficiently to warrant being placed under a local board as a local government area in its own right; the 1891 census returned a population of 4,754 and four years later the Colwyn Bay & Colwyn Urban District Council was incorporated. In 1901 the population was 8,689 and growing rapidly, swallowing up as suburbs Old Colwyn, Llandrillo yn Rhos and the headland to the west known as Rhos-on-Sea.

Contemporary with the promotion of the Great Orme Tramway in Llandudno was the idea of linking that town with Colwyn Bay by a direct tramway or light railway, since the London & North Western Railway route via the Llandudno branch (opened in 1858) to Llandudno Junction and then along the main Chester-Holyhead line to Colwyn Bay was decidedly circuitous. A more direct route had the advantage of passing through the principal built-up areas, thus tapping potential traffic at source. This idea was first mooted during the early 1890s, gaining momentum as a result of the 1896 Light Railways Act. Things now started to move quickly; interested local parties, headed by George Griffiths, applied in December of that year for a light railway order to construct 4½ miles of 3ft 6in gauge electric tramway between Llandudno and Colwyn Bay at an estimated cost of over £28,000. The application, heard at Colwyn Bay on 23 February 1897, was rejected on the grounds that the interests of the local landowners and Llandudno Corporation had not been sufficiently considered.

The next move came on 9 May 1897 when the Light Railway & General Construction Co Ltd was registered, to construct the proposed line, with a nominal capital of 75,000 Ordinary shares and an equal number of 6% Cumulative Preference shares. The four directors were J. Eckersley, D. R. Gibb, E. Hewitt and T. H. Fitzsimmons; the secretary was J. Morris and the registered office in Manchester. At the same time the company applied to the Light Railway Commissioners for the necessary light railway order, meeting to approve the draft order on 30 August 1897. The application was for authorisation to construct a total of 8 miles 25.45 chains of light railway, as one line, from Colwyn Bay over Penrhyn Hill (the landward side of the Little Orme) to Llandudno and from there southwards to Deganwy railway station on the LNWR's Llandudno branch at the mouth of the Conway estuary. The gauge proposed was 3ft 6in with working by animal power or electricity. Estimated cost was just over £65,000.

The public inquiry into the application was held by the commissioners in Colwyn Bay on 12 November 1897; their decision was deferred on account of the declared opposition of Llandudno UDC which stated that an application had been made for a Board of Trade provisional tramway order to construct part of the proposed line (2 miles 65 chains) itself. The commissioners however eventually decided in favour of the LR & GC Co and their approval was confirmed on 2 June 1899 by the

Board of Trade in the shape of the Llandudno and Colwyn Bay Light Railway Order, 1898. In addition to the above-mentioned contents of the Order, the following points are especially important since this Order provided the basis for the subsequent construction of the tramway: three years were allowed for the compulsory purchase of the land needed and for the completion of the works; electric traction was permitted and, under Section 76 of the Order, the sum of £2,980 had to be paid into court by the company before it could exercise its given powers. (Section 77 provided for the repayment of this deposit when the line was opened.)

This initial flurry of activity over, the scheme entered a new phase of procrastination, promises and pleading that lasted five years before anything concrete was achieved. At the bottom of it all was a simple matter of time and money – or, more correctly, a lack of those two commodities. (Legal and other costs had already amounted to £17,000 by the end of 1899; two years later the sum had risen to £25,000.) As the raising of capital proved a slower process than had originally been envisaged, the company was forced to spend money in purchasing time extensions just to retain its powers. Nor was the situation helped by the attitude of those who were in a position to speed up the proceedings. As the *Caernarvon & Denbigh Herald* of 23 August 1901 declared in a leading article:

> The petulant obstruction, the policy of opposition by the council, the exorbitant demands of Lord Mostyn, and the thousand and one claims made by adjacent local authorities nearly defeated the promotion of the movement by piling on heavy floating expenditure.

Under the 1898 Order the date for completion was 2 June 1902; with nothing at all begun an extension of time was applied for in November 1901. The Light Railway Commissioners held their inquiry in Colwyn Bay on 5 March 1902 and approved the application for this and also for a ½ mile deviation within Colwyn Bay. (This provided a slightly different route from Rhos-on-Sea up Rhos Road and across the fields, skirting rather than crossing the estate of Sir George Cayley, before joining the 1898 route over the LNWR line and down Princes Road, passing close to the railway station before terminating at the eastern end of Bay View Road.) While awaiting the Board of Trade's confirmation of the order the company – by now known as the Llandudno, Colwyn Bay, & Rhyl Electric Traction Co Ltd – paid into court the £2,980 specified in Section 76 of the 1898 Order. This meant that the company was only now in a position to carry out its undertaking – with no time left to start, let alone finish the work!

Not until 26 September, when the Board of Trade confirmed the Llandudno and Colwyn Bay Light Railway (Deviation and Amendment) Order, 1903, was the LCB & RET Co officially granted extra time; that for the purchase of land was increased to 4 years 6 months and the time for completion of the works altered to 5 years instead of 3 years and

> Provided that if the actual construction of the railway of 1898 be not substantially commenced by the thirtieth day of September 1903 the powers of the Company under the Order of 1898 and this Order shall cease.

A further provision was that Rhos Road could not be used by trams until that section of the highway occupied by the light railway had been widened in accordance with an agreement dated 15 December 1902 with the local landowner, Sir George Cayley. Presumably this work was never done as this section of the route was later altered (because of the expense involved in the widening?); it appears though that all the land for the line between Rhos-on-Sea and West Parade, Llandudno, was purchased within the new time limit. The route onwards from Rhos through Colwyn Bay was not regarded as satisfactory and alternative plans were drawn up. As for the promise included in the company's title of reaching Rhyl, no attempts were ever made to obtain powers for such a line and, as will be seen below, the promise quickly evaporated.

The LCB & RET Co was now in something of a sorry state. Only 11,560 shares had been issued, of which Thomas

Page 110: The L & CBER: *(top)* newly-constructed reserved section at Penrhynside; *(above)* one of the original 1907 cars poses before the opening of the line.

S. Turnbull, the company's one director, held 1,000. Of the remaining £10,560 subscribed capital, 9,530 shares were held by the Welsh Electric Traction Co. But – in refutation of a statement made by the company's solicitor in March 1902 that 'the company had done no work, nor purchased a yard of land, and that practically all the money had been spent' – things were now about to happen.

OPEN AT LAST

On 10 October 1903 the *North Wales Chronicle* announced that work on the tramway was at long last underway; at the end of September a start had been made near Rhos on a reserved section about 1,000yd long. A total of thirty-three men were engaged in filling-in and raising the route of the trackbed to the required level, erecting fences and laying sleepers. Stone for the work was obtained from a nearby quarry – nine men and eight carts were reported to be occupied in this work. From certain other contemporary events it is clear that the move to begin construction was merely political. Llandudno UDC was at the time again preparing to apply for a Board of Trade order to build its own tramway in Llandudno and the surveyor had already been instructed to modify the 1897 plans accordingly. Furthermore, on 26 September Cayley had written to the UDC requesting that the council joined him in petitioning the Board of Trade to stop the progress of the tramway; he claimed that the work done was not sufficient to be deemed a substantial commencement under the terms of the 1903 Order. It was, in short, a very lightly laid line to serve Mr W. Horton's brick works!

The LCB & RET Co continued its customary policy of uttering reassuring noises at every opportunity. Mr W. G. Rhodes, of the engineers retained for the construction, Messrs Hewitt & Rhodes of Manchester, had a meeting with the UDC and confidently stated that 'although he did not anticipate that the railway would be in full working order till Whitsuntide next', he thought that part might be. Towards the end of October the council surveyor inspected the work done and reported that forty-four men were engaged upon it and that 250yd or so of track had been well laid – the previously condemned sleepers having been replaced!

At the beginning of November the surveyor again visited the site and reported that the trackbed had been prepared for a distance of 800yd, seventy men were now employed and large quantities of rails and sleepers had been delivered. Horton was now financing the work and all in all it seemed as if the tramway was fast becoming fact. By January 1904 Rhos Road had been reached and crossed, for Colwyn Bay UDC received complaints about the tramway track there. The rails were supposed to lie flush with the road surface but had instead been laid 'on sleepers with shingles from the beach' heaped around them.

On 10 March 1904 *Tramway and Railway World* happily announced that Messrs Hewitt & Rhodes had secured the contract (which was worth £99,440) with the company, now entitled the Llandudno & Colwyn Bay Electric Traction Co, for the construction of the line from Mostyn Street, Llandudno, to Rhos-on-Sea. It was to be completed by 1 May and, according to that journal, 1½ miles had already been laid on that section while work on a new contract was being commenced by subcontractors. The truth was sadly different. At the beginning of June the company applied to the Board of Trade for another year's extension; the existing deadline expired on Thursday 2 June. Track had been laid for 365yd.

Colonel P. V. von Donop heard the company's application for a further time extension on Friday 15 July in the Colwyn Bay Hotel. Reporting on the meeting the *Chronicle* of 23 July stated that only two men were engaged on building the line. According to the newspaper account the contract for the line had in fact been placed on 25 April with the Welsh Electric Traction Co Ltd ('laughter'): 'The contract would be sublet for the construction because the company was not a constructing company (laughter).' Apparently £40,000 of fresh financial backing was to be provided by a London group, the Tramways Extension Syndicate, and this induced the Board of Trade to grant a time extension until 23 February 1905 with the possibility of a further six months to complete and open the line if the work was progressing satisfactorily. The construction contract was due to expire on 1 May 1905.

It must have come as no surprise to anyone when 1 May 1905 came and went without any further work having been done on the tramway. The story now takes on a familiar ring as the promotors continued to spend what capital they could raise on raising more capital and arranging time-extensions to buy more time to raise more capital to buy more time . . . and all the while the local councils grew more and more irate on the outside of this vicious circle. Then in 1906 the circle broke when the L & CBET Co went into liquidation; as a stop-gap measure to salvage the company's powers a nominal company, the Carnarvonshire Electric Traction Syndicate Ltd was formed until a new start could be made. This came on 25 July 1906 with the registration of the Llandudno & District Electric Tramway Construction Co Ltd, set up to adopt agreements with the L & CBET Co, the CETS and the Edinburgh firm of Bruce Peebles & Co Ltd to take over the necessary powers, issue contracts for the work and equipment, complete and actually operate the line. One wonders just what the local residents expected to come of it all!

This time though the move was destined to succeed. The L & DETC Co got off to a good start from the very beginning; 964 of its 1,000 £100 shares were immediately issued, A. B. Macartney was appointed as the first company secretary and the registered office set up in London. The four directors, Stephen Sellon (chairman), T. Stoker, R. S. Portheim and R. A. Freemantle promptly placed a contract with Bruce Peebles & Co, a firm already experienced in the field of tramway construction. Work pushed ahead on preparing the trackbed and early in 1907 tracklaying recommenced. In January two cars were brought to the site for trials on the line. These had originally been built for another Peebles contract (Canvey Island) but had since returned to the manufacturer. (Further details of these cars are given in Chapter 8.)

In startling contrast to the on-off-on efforts of the previous years, construction went forward at what must have seemed an incredible rate. Under the supervision of Peebles' engineer, Mr

W. B. Waite, and his assistant engineer, Mr E. Scholfield, the trackbed had been blasted out over the lower slopes of the Little Orme at Penrhynside, track laid, wiring erected. Within a matter of months a single line (with passing loops being added) stretched from the depot at Rhos-on-Sea to the West Shore, Llandudno, and the dual overhead wiring was in place. Grooved tramway rails were used, spiked to wooden sleepers and ballasted (paved over on the roadway sections), while the overhead wires were supported on a mixture of bracket arms and span wires. Current at 500–550Vdc was supplied by Llandudno UDC.

Arrangements for working the line were not neglected. A fleet of fourteen single-deck trams were ordered from the Midland Railway Carriage & Wagon Co, Mr W. H. Moorhouse (of tramway experience at Tynemouth and Barnsley) was appointed general manager, S. Sellon (formerly a member of the Board of Trade Committee on Light Railways and engineer to the British Electric Traction Co) was appointed chief engineer and a staff of men with at least two years' tramway experience recruited. Col von Donop inspected the portion of the line as completed on behalf of the Board of Trade on 26 September 1907 and found it basically satisfactory; the opening was set for October. On Thursday 17 of that month the first passenger-carrying trips were made by the new cars, though the occasion was a private affair for the benefit of the company officials and guests. With those making the trip over the line was a party of LNWR officials, Messrs Waite and Scholfield of Bruce Peebles and Messrs G. W. Stevenson and A. W. Thomas of the car builders. Two days later, Saturday 19 October, the line opened to the general public with cars starting simultaneously from both ends. The opening was in keeping with the history of the project with no ceremony (other than cheers and bell-ringing from spectators), a limited half-hourly service and one of the two cars (No 11) sticking on Penrhyn Hill. Nevertheless 4,434 passenger journeys were made that day and over £45 taken in receipts. The first ticket issued was purchased by Councillor J. McMaster.

EXPANSION . . .

Full scheduled services were instituted in November 1907 but modified the following month so that all cars terminated in Gloddaeth Avenue at the Llandudno end of the line instead of proceeding through to West Shore. This arrangement was stated by the company to give a quicker service with resulting benefits to the public; the cars would go through to Dale Street again in the summer when traffic warranted it.

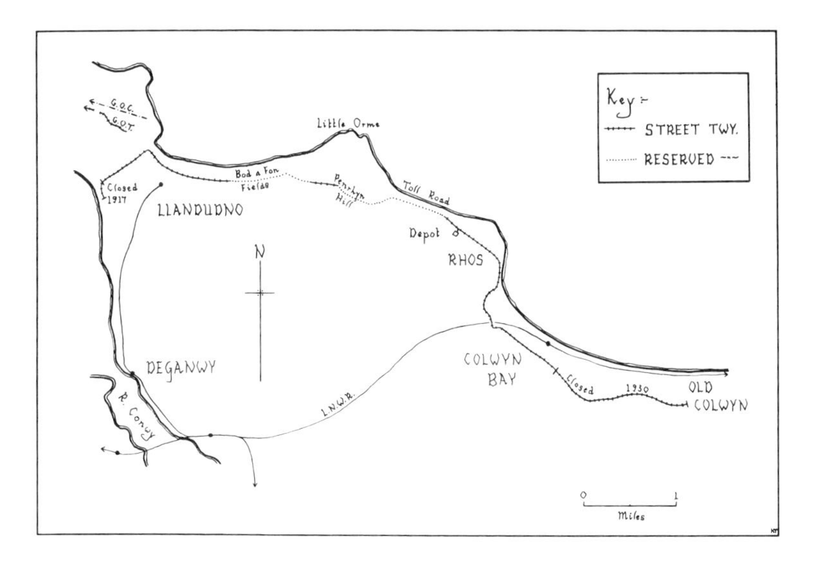

10 The Llandudno & Colwyn Bay Electric Railway

In November 1906 the L & DETC Co had applied to the Light Railway Commissioners for another light railway order, partly to provide an extension of time and partly to alter the proposed route of the tramway. The Order, confirmed by the Board of Trade on 30 September 1907, was entitled the Llandudno and Colwyn Bay Light Railway (Extension and Amendment) Order, 1907 – a title that aptly summed up its contents. Under its provisions the former route planned for Colwyn Bay under the Orders of 1898 and 1903 was abandoned in favour of $2\frac{1}{2}$ miles of new line from the bottom of Penrhyn Avenue at

Rhos, along the Promenade, up Whitehall Road, over the Chester-Holyhead railway by the road bridge into Conway Road (the A55) and hence to its continuation, Abergele Road, at the eastern side of the town. This new route was the one eventually constructed; a $\frac{1}{4}$ mile loop from Conway Road down Penrhyn Road towards the station, then back up Station Road to Abergele Road was included as a last attempt to reach the station but powers to construct this line were allowed to lapse.

Time allowed for completion of the works was extended under the Order to two years for the new lines, though construction of the last 50 chains of the line, from Station Road loop down Abergele Road, was not allowed to start until the company had secured powers for a full extension to Old Colwyn. An allowance of three years was given for the whole tramway; 12 months were allowed for the company to widen Rhos Road to 42ft (failing which £2,500 was to be paid to the local authority to do it). A further £3,000 was to be paid directly for two widenings in Abergele Road. Continuing its new dynamic policy of actually getting things done, the company immediately commenced work on the Colwyn Bay route with an Easter 1908 date set for the opening. By March of that year construction was well under way and it seemed that the date would be met but completion of the final touches delayed the introduction of public services until 7 June. Total route mileage was now 6.6 miles.

Now that it had at long last become a reality the tramway was handsomely meeting the expectations of its long-suffering supporters. The first general meeting of the L & DETC Co had been held, under the chairmanship of Sellon, on 24 March 1908 and receipts for 21 weeks (up to 13 March) of £1,542 announced – an average taking of over £72 per week throughout the non-tourist season. Car miles were reported as 46,400 and the total number of passenger journeys 174,664. That the concern was proving relatively prosperous was of little doubt; 21 April 1909 saw the company register a new, less cumbersome name – the Llandudno & Colwyn Bay Electric Railway Ltd. More tangible evidence of prosperity came later in the year when, in September, a further four single-deck cars were purchased as new (see Chapter 8 for details) from the United Electric Car Co, bringing the stock total to an impressive eighteen. During the year a loop was laid at the corner of Mostyn Street and Gloddaeth Street as part of the provision of a better service programme. Board of Trade returns for this period are given below.

Year ending November	*Working expenditure*	*Gross receipts*	*Passengers*
1908	£6,467	£12,217	1,060,281
1909	£10,001	£14,869	1,356,323

The fortunes of the L & CBER had not escaped the notice of another new company in the tramway world: Balfour, Beatty & Co Ltd. This firm had been set up in 1909 by its two joint managing directors, George Balfour and A. H. Beatty, to act as general and electrical engineers, contractors and operating managers for tramways, railways, lighting and power undertakings. In line with its policy of buying a sizeable interest in suitable concerns, such an interest was purchased in the L & CBER Ltd and Balfour took a seat on the board in 1910. (Apart from Balfour, Beatty & Co, he held directorships of twelve other concerns already and was a member of the council of the Tramways and Light Railways Association.)

In terms of public relations, by 1911 the honeymoon was over and the old familiar company-authority antagonism was back again. This time it was to stay until the tramway closed nearly half a century later – and then even beyond that. While the line continued to develop, in this instance by doubling its track through Rhos, complaints began to be voiced concerning the state of the track elsewhere. The Colwyn Bay surveyor was instructed by the council to draw up a report on the condition of the line through the borough so that representations could be made to the Board of Trade; the company promised that the necessary repairs would be carried out by Easter. Complaints were also received from the public about the screeching of cars round the tight corner from Mostyn Street into Gloddaeth Street; assurances were given that this would be reduced by greasing the rails. (The problem of noise at this corner dogged the tramway throughout its life and was never really solved. At a meeting of the Llandudno UDC in March 1911 the sound was referred to by one member as like 'the shrieks of Kilkenny cats'.) That same year, on the evening of 22 June, two illuminated cars were run to celebrate the coronation of King George V.

Moves to complete the extension to Old Colwyn were now coming to a head. The application for a light railway order for the line had originally been made in May 1907 for a one mile extension costing £5,870. The decision of the Light Railway Commissioners on this extension had been continually delayed, pending the outcome of a protracted dispute between the tramway company and Colwyn Bay UDC over the necessary road widening which would be entailed. While the dispute dragged on a series of time extensions were successfully sought from the Board of Trade for the last section of the lines authorised under the 1907 Order; these were granted on 17 September 1909, 21 September 1910, 29 September 1911 and 23 November 1911, giving an expiration date of 30 November 1912.

In March 1911 the L & CBER Co put the blame for the delay upon Colwyn Bay UDC, saying that an offer of £3,000 to cover the cost of the road widening had been refused and that other obstacles had been placed in the company's way. For its part the UDC denied this and stated that the sum offered was not sufficient to cover the costs involved – and besides, it was still owed £3,000 for road widenings carried out under the 1907 Order! By October the UDC was seriously considering construction of the extension itself as it regarded the then terminus at the top of Station Road as dangerous – especially since trams stood there illegally at night without displaying lights. The matter was finally resolved by the Light Railway Commissioners with the granting of the Llandudno and Colwyn Bay Light Railway (Extension No. 2) Order, 1912, confirmed on 1 August, which authorised the construction of a 1 mile 6.22 chains extension down Abergele Road from the end of the 1907 authorised line to the junction with Queens Road. Three years were allowed for the completion of the line, during the construction of which Abergele Road was to be widened to 24ft

Page 119: The L & CBER: *(above)* a busy moment at Hooson's Corner in Llandudno with Nos 2 and 5 (ex-Accrington) and 15 (ex-Bournemouth) *(D. W. K. Jones)*; *(below)* three of the withdrawn 1909 cars beside Rhos Depot; roof of 1907 car on left. *(D. W. K. Jones)*

wherever narrower than that, plus a footpath width of at least 6ft. Construction of the extension was somewhat slow by the company's previous standards and the new line did not open until 26 March 1915. Total route mileage was now 8.35 miles. Work was delayed by the track doubling programme which took priority; by the end of 1911 double track had reached the eastern side of Penrhyn Hill and was within 50yd of the loop at the summit.

. . . AND CONTRACTION

With the eastern end of the line having reached a successful conclusion, it is time to travel to the other terminus and look at the state of affairs there. As described in the previous section, the 1898 Order authorised the line to continue from Llandudno to Deganwy; as constructed however the tramway, after reaching the end of Gloddaeth Avenue at the West Shore, turned expectantly southwards along West Parade only to come to an abrupt halt – like the roadway itself – some 300yd further on opposite the end of Dale Street. Like the rest of the line in Llandudno at that time, this section was single track, interrupted by a short loop at one end and a two-track terminus at the other. Powers to construct the Deganwy extension had never been formally abandoned and time extensions had automatically been granted along with those for other sections of the tramway. The truth was, however, that any passenger traffic between Llandudno and Deganwy would have been a very poor second by comparison with that between Llandudno and Colwyn Bay; there was in addition a direct railway link between the two places. Capital expenditure was therefore directed in more profitable directions and once the extension to Old Colwyn was finished the line was regarded as complete. Powers to construct the Deganwy extension were accordingly permitted to lapse and in 1917 the West Parade section was removed as an economy measure, bringing the route mileage down to 8.14 miles.

The tramway now settled down to a fairly uneventful existence for the next dozen years or so, the only major happening being the purchase in 1920 of four open toastrack cars from English Electric (see Chapter 8), bringing the stock total to twenty-two. These cars were especially popular during the summer with visitors – though only when the weather was fine! General improvements were also continued throughout this period and the track doubling programme was completed; twin tracks now stretched from Colwyn Bay to Mostyn Street, Llandudno. The last section of line so treated was the stretch from the railway bridge to the council offices in Conway Road, Colwyn Bay. The opportunity to carry out the work came in 1929 after the UDC had widened the road. (It should perhaps be noted in passing that from 1 April 1926 Colwyn Bay & Colwyn Urban District was retitled Urban District of Colwyn Bay; on 20 September 1934 Colwyn Bay was incorporated as a Borough and during the charter week celebrations one of the trams was specially decorated and, in the words of the *North Wales Pioneer* of 25 September 1934, 'evoked well-merited praise'.)

Looking back from our modern-day vantage point it is not difficult to see that this period held the key to the future of the tramway. Events which took shape then were directly responsible for the eventual demise of the line a quarter of a century later, for in these pre-Second World War years came the assertion of the motor bus for a place in the scheme of things. To anyone acquainted with the broad outlines of tramway history this turn of events will be familiar – witness the similar story in the case of the Wrexham tramway. Motor buses had been licensed by Llandudno UDC from the early years of the twentieth century. They were operated by a firm known as the Llandudno & Motor Garage Co Ltd; by World War I the Llandudno Coaching Co Ltd and Messrs Jarvis & Woodyatt had joined in and applications for more licences increased.

Competition for the L & CBER between Llandudno and Colwyn Bay, and within those two towns, was inevitable. In 1926 Colwyn Bay UDC (possibly still with memories of lost skirmishes with the tramway company) obtained powers in a general Act of Parliament to operate buses in the borough; not to be caught on the hop the L & CBER Ltd began to consider running its own bus services but in 1929 was forced to announce a tactical withdrawal. In the face of private competition, and the increasing difficulties of operating through the holiday traffic along a narrow section of the main North Wales coast road (the A55), the decision was taken to curtail tram services at the end of the double track section at the Greenfield Road-Conway Road junction. From 22 September 1930 the single track section to Old Colwyn was abandoned and Crosville Motor Services Ltd stepped in smartly to fill the gap. The tramway company however had the foresight to obtain a licence to run buses if ever the tramway was forced by unforseen circumstances to close. The line now consisted, in its final form, of 5.72 miles of double and 0.82 miles of single track.

Crosville at this time was busy strengthening its hold on the bus services of the area; on 1 May 1930 it took over Brook Bros of Rhyl, on 1 August North Wales Silver Motors and on 18 February of the following year, the Llandudno Coaching & Carriage Co. It must have started to become clear at that time that the trams would, sooner or later, be displaced by buses. The fact that it was later rather than sooner was simply due to the cost involved in resurfacing the roadway after the removal of the tracks; this same obstacle effectively blocked the company's 1931 proposal to replace the trams with trolleybuses, as was current Balfour, Beatty policy, thus retaining use of the overhead equipment. It was decided instead to continue with the trams, replacing most of the existing ailing stock with second-hand cars from other systems. In 1932 and 1933 five single-deck cars were purchased from Accrington Corporation and in 1936 ten double-deck cars were bought from Bournemouth. (Board of Trade permission to use double-deck vehicles between Old Colwyn and Penrhyn Bay had been obtained in 1916; this was now extended to the whole system provided that no passengers were carried on the open upper decks over the exposed stretch of the line at Penrhyn Bay and Penrhynside if the wind speed exceeded 50mph.)

On the face of it the tramway was enjoying a period of reasonable prosperity: it had a new manager (W. G. Hamilton of Bournemouth from 1931), a second source of power (Colwyn

Bay's new power station opened in 1932 and current for the Colwyn Bay section of the line was now taken from here), new wiring (in 1938 the entire overhead was renewed) and a fleet of 'new' cars. The real truth was slightly different; an important section of line had been abandoned, only ten year old (or more) cars could be afforded and, when all was said and done, it was only the cost of abandonment that was keeping the line open. The special circumstances of the war years about to come merely warded off the inevitable a little longer.

THE WAR YEARS

Throughout the duration of World War II the tramway continued its uninterrupted run of daily operation, the only direct effect of hostilities being the blacking-out of the tram windows and the use of blue bulbs for internal lighting in accordance with blackout regulations. Indirectly the war had many effects upon the tramway – the principal one being a welcome increase in passenger figures arising from the influx to the area of several Government offices and service personnel. A further bounty was traffic deserting to the tramway from the reduced bus services – one of the casualties of petrol rationing. Another result of rationing was the introduction of various special services, one of which was a 'staff car' for employees returning home after evening duties. Another was an extra shuttle service (the 'Llandudno Local') between the West Shore and Craig y Don. Still another was the hiring of cars on Sundays for private excursions. The last major change brought by the war was one repeated on countless other tramway systems in Britain – the employment of conductresses.

Although never on the receiving end of any war damage, three incidents occurred on the tramway which need mention. The first took place in the spring of 1943 when gales and heavy seas caused the collapse of the old sea wall beside the reserved track along Penrhyn Bay between the Little Orme and Rhos. Several tons of debris were deposited on the line. (Similar though less damaging events had occurred in 1927 and 1933 and, as will be seen, this stretch of line was to become a notorious trouble spot.) In October 1945 exactly the same thing happened only this time with more serious results; the track formation was so undermined that the seaward track of the two was declared unsafe and for two weeks, while the damage was repaired, single line working was in force over the inner track between the crossovers at Penrhynside and the depot. The third and final incident took place in November of the same year when car No 16 (originally No 6 of 1907) ran a hot axlebox, caught fire and was scrapped.

POST-WAR PROBLEMS

The tramway emerged from the war years in optimistic mood, promptly ordering in 1946 two secondhand double-deck cars from Darwen Corporation. These were of a far more modern design than anything possessed by the L & CBER (they dated from just before the war) and were awarded new numbers of 23 and 24. They were to be the last items of rolling stock to come to the line. After regauging, trials, driver training etc, a Ministry of Transport test was held on the cars on 14 April 1948 with an outcome that came both as a shock and a disappointment to the company; because of their high-sided, closed bodies the new cars would not be permitted to operate in public service on the section through Bod a Fon Fields, over Penrhyn Hill, along the coastal stretch and on to the depot at Rhos because of the possible danger of overturning in windy conditions. Consequently No 23 entered service on Thursday 22 April on the Llandudno local service between Nant y Gamar Road and West Shore, followed by No 24 on a similar shuttle service between the depot and Colwyn Bay terminus.

Meanwhile the never-ending task of maintaining permanent way to the required standard continued; the first major section to be tackled after the war was that through Rhos from the depot to Colwyn Crescent. One track was relaid at a time, resulting in single line working throughout 1946–7. For some reason one track was relaid on a new concrete bed and the other on ballasted sleepers (to facilitate possible future singling?), both then being metalled over.

During the winter of 1948–9 the track along Penrhyn Bay was again damaged by heavy seas, again the ground under the seaward track was washed away and single line working was put into operation while the formation was repaired. This time new crossovers were laid at Maesgwyn Road and the Golf House at each end of the affected section to reduce disruption of normal services to a minimum. Four winters later, 1952–3, the story was repeated yet again. After a start had been made to make a more solid defence against the sea by hauling boulders up the beach with a winch fitted to car No 17, the attempt was abandoned as too difficult and too costly. From then on only the nearside track was used between the two loops and a single overhead wire was installed using poles and bracket arms acquired from Stockport Corporation in 1951 as spares. The outer track was left to disappear under piles of shingle and suffer piecemeal destruction in the construction of a new sea wall.

The ex-Stockport poles were not the only secondhand items to be purchased for the tramway to replace aged and failing equipment. In November 1952 more tubular poles, a number of wheel tyres and several items of depot equipment were bought from Birmingham Corporation; the following year a number of Dick, Kerr type 30B motors, gears, axles and wheels, and a quantity of seat cushions were obtained from the same source. In 1954 four sets of Dick, Kerr K4 controllers came from Sunderland Corporation. (See Chapter 8 for details of modifications to the L & CBER cars.)

Several minor track alterations took place during the early 1950s. In November 1952 the single line section in Mostyn Street was lifted and relaid; while this work was in progress cars for Colwyn Bay commenced their journey from Mostyn Broadway with West Shore being served by a shuttle car from Gloddaeth Street. Autumn 1953 saw resleepering of the reserved section between Nant y Gamar Road and Penrhyn Hill, the transfer of the trailing crossover from the Colwyn Crescent end of Penrhyn Avenue in Rhos to Mostyn Broadway and the laying of a sewer under the Rhos end of the toll road. (While this latter work was being carried out passengers and crew

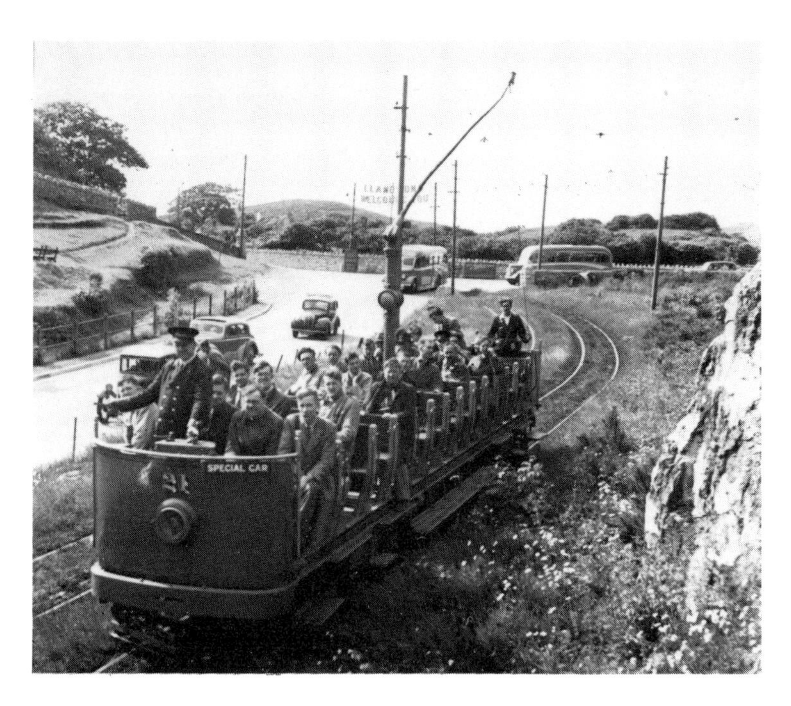

Page 126: The L & CBER: *(above)* toastrack No 21 descending Penrhyn Hill *(D. W. K. Jones)*; *(below)* Rhos Depot with toastracks 19 and 21, 1907 car No 18 (the renumbered 11) and No 24 (ex-Darwen). *(D. W. K. Jones)*

walked over the break to change cars.) The crossover was moved to provide more flexible facilities to deal with a much-needed increase in traffic; cars could now terminate in Mostyn Broadway by the Grand and Arcadia Theatres and pick up the returning crowds bound for Colwyn Bay. Following complaints by the council in 1953 over the state of the track and roadways in Llandudno the company gave an assurance that future repairs would be more substantial; in 1954 sections of Mostyn Broadway were relaid and retarred.

The problem of the Penrhyn Bay sea wall, however, still loomed large. In the summer of 1953 the local authorities involved were given a government grant to construct a new set of sea defences and a new sea wall. This work was carried out during 1953; after its completion a public inquiry was held at the beginning of 1954 to hear objections from the L & CBER and local residents. The latter claimed that the cost of the work had been excessive and for the money spent a promenade could easily have been incorporated into the structure; the tramway company on the other hand claimed that it *was* the authorities' intention to construct a new coast road along the sea wall, thus depriving the company of its tolls collected on the existing roadway. In reply the authorities denied any intent to construct a new road but carefully left their options open by admitting that the work done would facilitate any construction of a coast road at a later date. All of this added fuel to the company's growing belief that Llandudno UDC was anxious to see the back of the trams – hence the continual complaints about the state of the track and the roads.

The council was not the only body that would profit by the closure of the tramway. The chairman of the L & CBER Ltd, Sir Joseph Nall, announced traffic figures for 1953 as follows:

Passengers:	2,744,593
Receipts:	£31,137
Loss:	£1,222

One hopes that Sir Joseph – to give him his full title, Colonel Sir Joseph Nall, DSO, TD, DL, JP, M Inst T – gained some small measure of satisfaction from his being created a baronet in the New Year's Honours List for on 10 November 1954 he announced even worse figures for that year:

Passengers:	2,697,994
Receipts:	£30,906
Loss:	£3,004

In view of the current financial state of the company the directors were actively considering replacing the trams with motor buses. Appeals and proposals by tramway enthusiasts that a preservation body should step in, or that Llandudno UDC should purchase the line and run it for a summer season only – in much the same way as the Great Orme line – were made in a valiant but (as it soon became plain) futile effort to save the last 3ft 6in electric tramway – and the last privately-owned surviving tramway – in the country from closure.

CLOSURE

On 14 September 1955 came the long-expected announcement: the tramway was definitely to close before the year was out. To add weight to the decision a secondhand bus was purchased from the East Kent Road Car Co for the purpose of training drivers. Circumstances however dictated otherwise and it became apparent that the trams would, after all, see in the New Year. That closure would be delayed was made evident on 12 October when the chairman of the North Western Area Traffic Commissioners declared that the L & CBER Ltd would have to agree upon a joint bus timetable with Crosville and then have it approved by the commissioners before the tramway's bus service could begin.

The second delay came on 1 November when a meeting was held in Colwyn Bay to decide the future of the track and roads used by the tramway. Representatives of the company, the local authorities and the Ministry of Transport were present. The outcome of the meeting was that no decision could as yet be reached as to who was responsible for making good the roadways, though the local authorities remained unmoved from their conviction that, under the original 1898 Light Railway Order, the onus rested fairly and squarely on the tramway company.

At the same time it became imperative from the company's point of view to cease operation before the summer of 1956. The reason was simply financial: the company's contract with the Merseyside & North Wales Electricity Board for the supply of current for the overhead was due to expire then. MANWEB presented the company with two choices after the contract expired: either pay a new charge of £100 per day for the supply or take over the generating plant from MANWEB and install it behind the depot. (It should be noted that MANWEB employed a full-time staff of eight men to operate this plant.) Neither of these alternatives was within the existing financial means of the company and a closure date of Saturday 24 March 1956 was promptly announced. It was a case of cutting further losses as quickly as possible, then settling the thorny question of track removal. Eight cars were officially allocated for service during 1956 (three ex-Accrington and five ex-Bournemouth) while the rest of the fleet was to be withdrawn as soon as any maintenance became necessary. Two of the first to go were ex-Bournemouth cars Nos 9 and 10, scrapped in January.

And so the appointed day of closure arrived. Not surprisingly, the trams were packed to capacity all day with local residents, tramway enthusiasts and other visitors – including a party of former Bournemouth tram-drivers who had a chance to try their hands again at the controls of their old charges. The official part of the proceedings began with an evening cocktail party at the Imperial Hotel, Llandudno, hosted by the company's deputy chairman, Mr Stanley Dudman. Meanwhile the official 'last car', ex-Bournemouth No 8, was brought up from the depot under the guidance of driver Dick Hughes and conductor Bob Morgan – long-standing employees of 39 and 37 years service respectively. At 10.20pm the official party, consisting of representatives of the company, the local authorities, the police and Crosville Motor Services – totalling a hundred or so in all – clambered aboard No 8 outside the North Western Hotel on Mostyn Broadway. With Chief Inspector J. E. Woolley at the controls and watched by a large crowd of onlookers, the loaded tram moved off towards West Shore terminus.

Leaving West Shore to the strains of 'Auld Lang Syne' from the crowd, No 8 travelled back to the North Western Hotel and on through Llandudno towards the Little Orme. Here the chairman of Llandudno UDC, Councillor John Owen, took over the controls for the stretch up to the depot. No 8 paused here while the controls were handed over to the Mayor of Colwyn Bay, Councillor Edward Hughes, for the final run down to Greenfield Road terminus, followed by a wide assortment of other road users. The arrival at and subsequent departure from Colwyn Bay were witnessed by another large crowd and a second convoy made its way along behind No 8, this time returning to the depot. Passengers for Llandudno were taken on from there by one of the company's buses. So died the tramway.

EPILOGUE

Thus it was that on 25 March 1956 the L & CBER Co became a bus operator; its six double-deck buses ironically sported the tramway's original livery of maroon and cream as they plied their trade between Llandudno and Colwyn Bay, faithfully adhering to the former tramway route, deviating only slightly at the reserved sections of track. Not so faithfully adhered to was the agreement with Crosville over such small things as timetables which, according to the local authorities, residents and press, were chiefly remarkable for their absence.

Quickly Messrs Walter & Co of Oldham and Conway went about their contracted task of dismantling, destroying and generally disposing of the carcase of the tramway. Bournemouth Town Council expressed a willingness to purchase car No 6 (ex-Bournemouth No 85) – if the asking price of £75 could be raised. If a very generous and big-hearted Mr A. Richardson of Rhyl had not stepped in and bought the tram in question and promptly presented it to the Museum of British Transport at Clapham one wonders if the exceedingly slow-grinding wheels of local government would have saved No 6 from the fate of its shed mates. Stripped of anything of scrap value, anything saleable, the bodies were unceremoniously burnt outside the depot. All, that is, except Nos 23 and 24, the two ex-Darwin cars. Their steel bodies survived through the summer before receiving the scrapman's torch.

Although the overhead wires went within a month of the tramway's closure, the track lingered on – to the considerable annoyance of the local authorities (Llandudno UDC and Colwyn Bay Corporation) who wished to see its speedy removal. The reason for the delay was quite simple, the L & CBER Co did not have the money to pay for the lifting of the track and the subsequent restoration of the roads. The company claimed that if it *did* decide to lift the track (presumably its scrap value would cover the cost of this part of the operation) it saw no reason to make good the roads since – undeniably – their condition in that broken state would still be better than it was in 1906! The two councils were not unnaturally inclined to a somewhat different view and began to make threatening noises regarding seeking of powers to lift the track, repair the roads and hand the tramway company the bill. Whereupon the tramway company decided not to go out fighting and handed over £5,000 to the councils to do the whole job; this sum was effectively increased by the value of the track.

The subsequent roadworks occasioned minor alterations to the tramway company's bus route and services; the buses, known familiarly as the 'Red buses', were based at the former tram depot which had been adapted for the purpose. Greater problems arose from competition with Crosville and the smaller concern soon found itself being squeezed out of existence. In April 1961 the tramway company announced that it was giving up the struggle and the last L & CBER buses ran on 27 May. The following day the service was taken over by Crosville which had purchased the company's goodwill for £40,000.

There was now little reason for the continuing existence of the L & CBER Co Ltd. All that was left was the Penrhyn Bay toll road and in the face of the local authorities' desire to improve the public roads in the area to serve the growing residential development the company decided to dispose of its remaining assets. Accordingly, on 14 November 1961, the L & CBER Co went into voluntary liquidation, paying to the shareholders 10s (50p) per 10s preferred share and ¼d per 1s (5p) deferred share. There the story appeared to end with the tramway becoming a fading memory for all those who had known it. But it does not quite end there; on 19 September 1974 the Llandudno Tramway Society was formed to keep that memory alive by collecting relics of the line for an intended local transport museum. Although the society's plan to secure the return of No 6 to Llandudno has been defeated – at least for some time if not for ever – by the successful application by Bournemouth for custody of it following the 1973 closure of the museum at Clapham, the remains of ex-Northampton double-decker No 21 were acquired from a Northamptonshire farm in 1977 and moved to Llandudno for restoration. In October of the same year a quantity of original rails from the West Shore terminus were lifted by Aberconwy Borough Council and sold to the society. Although the search is still on for a suitable site, who knows, perhaps one day Llandudno will hear the sound of electric trams once again.

8 Working the L & CBER

THE ROUTE DESCRIBED

Before 1917 the western end of the tramway was on the actual West Parade itself, opposite the end of Dale Street. Two short tracks were provided at the terminus and a short passing loop was sited some 200yd or so down the line, just before it turned sharply right into Gloddaeth Avenue; otherwise this section was single track. From 1917 onwards the western terminus of the L &CBER was here at the end of Gloddaeth Avenue at its junction with West Parade, the 350yd of track along to Dale Street being lifted in that year.

From the west shore the line ran straight across the Great Orme isthmus down Gloddaeth Avenue (where there was a passing loop for a while) and Gloddaeth Street (another loop was sited here) before it swung abruptly right at Hooson's Corner into Mostyn Street. From 1909 a passing loop existed on the actual corner – the corner that gave rise to continual complaints about the squealing of trams as they rounded it. From here the single line ran down Mostyn Street for $\frac{1}{4}$ mile until it reached a point flanked by the Library and St John's Church where it doubled. (It should be borne in mind that in the first instance the line was laid entirely with single track lacking even benefit of any passing loops which were laid as and when it was felt they were needed.) The double track carried on through to the 1930 Colwyn Bay terminus, the work having been completed in a number of stages by that date.

Leaving Mostyn Street the double track entered that road's continuation, Mostyn Broadway, running past (on the right) the North Western Hotel and (on the left) what was later to be the Crosville bus depot and the Grand Theatre. Halfway between the North Western and the Grand was a trailing crossover and in 1953 a similar one was laid outside the theatre. Still sweeping along the main thoroughfare of Llandudno, the tramway passed into Mostyn Avenue, left the town centre for the outlying district of Craig y Don, and carried beyond the end of the highway into its first reserved section at the trailing crossover at Nant y Gamar Road.

The line then ran through Bod a Fon fields for $\frac{3}{4}$ mile, rising more steeply up the lower slopes of the Little Orme above Llandudno Bay. Reaching Bryn y Bia Road the tracks followed the side of the roadway for another $\frac{1}{4}$ mile to the summit of Penrhyn Hill (as this part of the Little Orme is known) at Penrhynside. Here began the 1 in $11\frac{1}{2}$ descent on reserved track to the left of and above the main Llandudno–Colwyn Bay road which had been crossed at the summit; and so down the hill, along the reserved section that was later to become part of Glan y Mor Road and onto the toll road on the open, trouble-prone stretch beside Penrhyn Bay. Here the golf clubhouse was passed on the right and the Toll House on the left before the line swung inland into Rhos-on-Sea down Penrhyn Avenue, reaching the depot and offices of the L & CBER on the right just before another trailing crossover at the junction of the avenue and Church Road. (Penrhyn Avenue was formerly known as Tramway Avenue.)

The tramway depot was situated on the landward side of the line which was connected to the Llandudno-bound track by two trailing points; the spur from each set of points led to four shed roads into the depot. As well as housing the trams at night, this was where all minor repairs, overhauls and repainting jobs were done. Also housed here were the various staff and general offices. A good indication of the strong rural character of much of the line is given by the fact that this now populous district was known, when the tramway arrived, as Klondyke, on account of its isolation!

The end of Penrhyn Avenue was reached $\frac{1}{2}$ mile beyond the depot; immediately before this (until 1935) a trailing crossover existed at Colwyn Crescent. At the end of Penrhyn Avenue the line curved right, in the centre of Rhos, to emerge onto the Promenade which it occupied for $\frac{1}{4}$ mile. Turning inland once again the tramway passed through the residential area on the border of Rhos and Colwyn Bay before crossing the main Chester-Holyhead railway line at Brompton Avenue bridge and joining Colwyn Bay's main thoroughfare, Conway Road (the A55). As the two tracks of the tramway reached the railway bridge they briefly became single for it never proved possible to double the line here. For the remaining mile to the 1930 terminus at the junction of Conway Road with Greenfield Road the track was again double – though for a short (200yd) stretch between the Council Offices and the top of Station Road the two tracks were interlaced on account of the narrowness of the roadway. Halfway between Station Road and the terminus, outside St Paul's Church, was the line's final trailing crossover.

Before 1930 the tramway had extended as a single line with three passing loops and a short double-track section along Abergele Road (the A55) to Old Colwyn, terminating by the Queens Hotel; as described in the previous chapter, this portion of the line closed on 21 September 1930 and was never reinstated.

Today the urban development which took place during the tramway's life continues unabated; Llandudno's housing estates now extend alongside the route of the line to West Parade and Craig y Don. As so often happens with tramways, as opposed to railways, traces of their erstwhile existence disappear quickly after closure and the case of the L & CBER is no exception. The street sections are now just streets with no hint that they were once more than that; the reserved sections have undergone a variety of changes. The Bod a Fon fields right of way has now reverted to the pasture from which it was taken with only a fence and hedge along one side of the decaying trackbed to indicate where the trams ran. A metal gate marks the point where the line crossed Nant y Gamar Road to enter the fields.

The reserved section on the descent of Penrhyn Hill towards Rhos has suffered even more: construction of a dual carriageway has completely obliterated the former trackbed next to the original road. Glan y Mor Road is now a built-up area, as is the old toll road – now just a promenade and public road. The old car shed remains and is now a BRS parcels depot; other than that Colwyn Bay, like Llandudno, has effectively removed all traces of the line that once served it so well.

ACCIDENTS

There is no reason to suppose that the L & CBER was not without its fair share of minor accidents; it does appear though to have been unlucky in being involved in at least three fatal incidents. The first occurred on Friday 28 June 1914 when ten-year-old Trevor Roberts of Penrhyn Bay was knocked down by a tram outside the Golf Club at Rhos-on-Sea. Trevor was employed after school hours as a caddie at the club and on the evening in question he walked out from behind a waiting tram and was hit by one approaching, apparently disregarding (or misinterpreting) the warning bell that rang in the clubhouse whenever a tram approached. The second accident involved a Holyhead woman, Dorothy Wall, who slipped and fractured her skull while trying to avoid a tram in Craig y Don on the evening of Thursday 9 February 1928.

The third fatality was again that of a child; this time a three-year-old boy was struck by a tram in Penrhyn Avenue on Friday 15 May 1936 as he ran after his ball. The tram was travelling at just 10mph but for a three-year-old child that was enough.

OPERATION

Services

The tramway's very first timetable, which came into effect from the line's opening, consisted of a service commencing from both ends (West Parade and Rhos Depot) at 9.00am and operating at 30 minute intervals. (Until the extension of the line into Colwyn Bay in 1908 passengers between there and Rhos were conveyed at 3d a time in horse-brakes by Messrs J. F. Francis & Sons, carriage proprietors of Colwyn Bay, under an agreement with the tramway company.) Journey time over the first section of the line was approximately 30min; with the extension to Colwyn Bay this increased to 40min and again to

Page 137: The L & CBER: *(above)* No 24 (ex-Darwen) on the railway bridge in Colwyn Bay *(D. W. K. Jones)*; *(below)* works car No 23 (ex-Bournemouth). *(D. W. K. Jones)*

50min when Old Colwyn was reached. After the closure of this last extension the time was back to roughly 40min – actual times varied between different scheduled workings by a few minutes. When fully operational the normal pattern was for a 10min interval service in the summer, reduced to 20min in the winter months. Interspersed with these were the two 'locals': shuttle services between West Parade and Nant y Gamar Road in Llandudno and between Rhos Depot and the terminus in Colwyn Bay.

Normal services commenced between 6.00am and 7.00am and finished between 10.00pm and 11.00pm (as with the actual schedules, these times were subject to endless minor variations over the years but serve to give the general picture). The first car of the day was a workmen's special; under the 1898 Order the company was required to run at least one car in each direction every day (except Sunday) before 7.00am and again after 5.30pm for the benefit of workmen who were to travel at a reduced rate.

Occasionally special charter trips were run, in early years for children's outings, and in later years for tramway enthusiasts.

Working

As would be expected, different patterns of working were in force at different times of the year. During the winter, with its reduced traffic and services, most of the work was done by the single-deck cars with the double-deckers filling out where need be. In the summer months all the double-deck cars would be in service, together with the toastracks, while the single-deckers stayed in reserve – though at the height of the season the whole fleet would be in action and the timetable abandoned!

Generally speaking each car – crewed by driver and conductor – would adhere to the timetable as far as possible; this usually meant a fairly continuous service from one terminus to the other and then almost immediately back again.

Fares

The original fare structure, as laid down by the 1898 Order, was based upon a maximum rate of 1d per mile or fraction thereof, though the company was permitted to charge 2d for any distance between ½ mile and two miles. The exception to this scale was the workmen's rate of ½d per mile (minimum 1d). Passengers were allowed 28lb of luggage free of charge; various rates otherwise applied at the discretion of the company for goods, since the tramway was authorised to carry minerals, parcels, animals and general goods.

The fare structure gave a basic end-to-end fare of 5d when the first section of the line opened; this increased to 8d (3½p) when the line was fully opened. During the late 1920s fare increases were authorised (1½d per mile ordinary, 1d per mile workmen's and an extra 75 per cent on the goods charges) but overall the change had little effect. Indeed, the through fare later dropped to 7d (3p) and was raised to 9d (3½p) only in 1953. Apart from these changes, and minor stage alterations, the fares were remarkably consistent throughout the life of the tramway. Children under 14 years travelled at half-price; children under three rode free. Special weekly tickets for schoolchildren and workmens were issued, as well as workmen's day returns; until 1941 a special 'excursion' return of 1s (5p) was available between Llandudno and Colwyn Bay. Tickets used were of the Bell Punch variety.

Tolls

The L & CBER Ltd charged a toll for use of the road section of the tramway along Penrhyn Bay. These tolls, for the return journey on the day of ticket issue only, were:

Perambulator, light handcart or pedal cycle	1d
Motor cycle on two wheels carrying one person	3d
Motor cycle combination, or carrying two persons	6d
Motor vehicle of seating capacity not exceeding eight passengers	1s
Cart or carriage drawn by one horse	1s
Light lorry or van not exceeding 5 tons gross loaded	1s
Cart or carriage drawn by two horses	1s 6d

Heavy lorries, coaches and other public service vehicles were prohibited from using the toll road – though when the company's own buses were introduced they used the road and from then on other PSVs were admitted upon payment of a charge of 2s 6d (12½p). As regards the procedure for using the road, the notice at the toll house detailing the above charges also gave the following instruction:

> Drivers of vehicles passing through this gate are respectfully requested to see that the Toll-gate Keeper punches, in their presence, a ticket representing the value of the toll paid.

ORIGINAL STOCK

Nos 1–14

The L & CBER's first fourteen cars were ordered and supplied in one batch for the opening of the line in 1907. Their bodies were constructed by the Midland Railway Carriage & Wagon Co Ltd of Shrewsbury and the running gear manufactured and fitted by Mountain & Gibson Ltd of Bury. The bodies were single-deck saloons with clerestory roofs, vestibuled end platforms with entrances each side, and eight drop windows on each side. Internally the saloon was divided into two compartments, both with longitudinal rattan seating. Total accommodation was given as forty-two. The original intention was to have one compartment for smokers and one for non-smokers but this idea was later dropped. (Judging by complaints made by members of the public the communicating door between the compartments was often left open or the division simply ignored anyway.)

Running gear consisted of a pair of four-wheel bogie trucks of the equal-wheel type, with two Bruce Peebles & Co split case 30hp motors mounted between the axles of each truck. The lifeguards were Mountain & Gibson's 'Simplex' type; sanding gear was Cummings and the magnetic brakes Westinghouse. (Hand wheels were also fitted for manually operating the brakes.) Current collection was originally by a single trolley pole but this was quickly found to be unsatisfactory and was subsequently replaced by two trolleys, mounted near the centre of the roof, facing outwards. No further alterations were made to the cars until 1924–5 when the original motors were replaced by BTH GE249 models and B49CC controllers and magnetic brakes fitted. In 1931 work started on filling-in one of the side entrances on the end platforms; at the close of the following summer season Nos 1–5 were withdrawn and scrapped (though six bogies survived for use with the ex-Accrington trams – see next section).

In 1936 Nos 6, 10, 11 and 14 were renumbered to follow consecutively from the ex-Accrington and Bournemouth cars (see next section) and became Nos 16, 19, 18 and 17 respectively. All the remaining 1907 cars were withdrawn and scrapped. Of the quartet of survivors No 19 was set aside for conversion to a toast-rack vehicle but was scrapped in 1937; 16 was scrapped after being damaged by fire in November 1945 while 17 and 18 survived until closure in 1956 (though by this time No 17 was out of use). Final modifications to these cars included the installation of lifeguards between the trucks and the permanent closure of the drop windows.

Nos 15–18

The second batch of cars ordered for the tramway were built in 1909 and delivered in September of that year by the United Electric Car Co Ltd of Preston. Running gear was again by Mountain & Gibson. The bodywork was unique for this country: a main saloon with fully-vestibuled end platforms, each with a seat for two passengers on the closed side opposite the entrance, and a clerestory roof. Sliding doors gave access to the saloon from the end platforms; one end of the saloon was partitioned-off to provide a smokers' compartment. Transverse seating in the saloon was for twenty-seven. Total body length was 31ft.

Running gear consisted of a four-wheel radial truck (Warner pattern), rheostatic and manually-operated (hand wheel) brakes. In 1927 all four cars were updated with the fitting of Peckham P35 trucks from Brush, new BTH control equipment and the addition of magnetic brakes.

The whole batch was withdrawn at the same time, 1936, and stored next to Rhos Depot until 1941 when the trucks were removed and sold to Leeds Corporation Transport Department. The bodies were subsequently disposed of – two going to an army camp at Rhyl.

Nos 19–22

The final batch of cars ordered for the tramway as new came in 1920 from the English Electric Co. They were identical completely open toastrack cars fitted with two English Electric (Mountain & Gibson pattern) equal-wheel bogie trucks. Each truck was powered by a BTH GE149 motor; control was by B18 DD controllers with hand wheel and magnetic braking systems. The lifeguards were of a fixed pattern, somewhat reminiscent of railway cowcatchers. Seating was for 60 arranged as follows: 7 lift-over bench seats, 1 half-width lift-over bench seat each side of the central trolley standard, 7 lift-over bench seats. The full-width seats held 4 passengers each, the half-width seats 2 each.

In 1936, with the renumbering of Nos 6, 10, 11 and 14 (see above), toastrack No 19 was temporarily renumbered 23 for a brief period until the former No 10 (now renumbered 19) was scrapped. In 1954 Nos 19 and 20 were fitted with K4 controllers obtained from Sunderland. All four cars were scrapped after closure in 1956 though several of the seats survive as station benches on the Fairbourne Railway.

Livery

Basic livery for the above cars was maroon below the waist, cream above, fully lined-out in gold. Nos 1–14 had the legend LLANDUDNO & COLWYN BAY in gold in the centre of the waist panels on each side while the car number was painted in gold above the electric headlight in the centre of the dash. Nos 15–18 carried the legend LLANDUDNO & COLWYN BAY ELECTRIC RAILWAY LIMITED along the whole length of the rocker panel on each side while the car number, again in gold, was painted on each side of the dash headlights. In the centre of each waist panel was the coat of arms insignia.

During World War I Nos 1–14 were painted battleship grey as a temporary measure but some cars continued to sport this colour until they were either withdrawn or repainted in the new official livery of green and cream in 1933 (as were the other original cars). At the same time official crests were added to the sides of the closed trams.

Indicators

Nos 1–14 were originally equipped with destination boards hung at the bottom of the windows in the centre of each side and at each end. Later – in line with the company's standard policy – roof boards were added on each side giving details of the complete route travelled. Those cars that had one side entrance enclosed on each platform had the front destination board moved to the nearside front window. Nos 15–18 were originally equipped with destination boxes on the roof at each end but they later disappeared and were replaced by standard route boards on each side and a metal destination sign hung in the nearside front window. The toastracks simply had one of these destination signs hung on the front dash.

During World War II all these signs and boards disappeared (the metal signs later reappeared) and it was not until the tramway's very final years that any other indicators were used – black-printed yellow paper strips above the windows of the closed cars. The toastracks had a destination strip stuck on the lower off-side of the dash.

SECONDHAND STOCK

Between 1932 and 1946, as already mentioned in the previous chapter, a total of seventeen secondhand cars were purchased by the L & CBER from three different municipal operators, Accrington, Bournemouth and Darwen. Instead of continuing the numbering scheme as 23, 24 and so on, these cars were renumbered to fill gaps in the existing fleet list – usually the gaps were caused by the withdrawal of cars to be replaced. Individual details of the cars are given below.

Nos 1–5

These were the 1920–2 ex-Accrington Brush built single-deck cars purchased in 1932–3 as replacements for the original L & CBER Nos 1–5. Their Accrington numbers were 28–32 respectively; Nos 29 and 32 were bought as complete cars while in the case of the other three only the bodies were acquired. These latter bodies were mounted on the six better condition trucks salvaged from the withdrawn Nos 1–5 to save the trouble and expense of buying and regauging more Accrington trucks than strictly necessary (the Accrington system having a 4ft gauge). Those bogies regauged on Nos 29 and 32 were Brush type C maximum-traction trucks fitted with Dick, Kerr 40hp 31B motors.

The car bodies were of the closed saloon pattern with one entrance on each vestibuled end platform; the single trolley was mounted centrally on the clerestory roof. Accommodation was on two longitudinal wooden benches. Both hand wheel and magnetic brakes were fitted.

During their new life at Llandudno the cars were subjected to several minor alterations, beginning with the immediate removal of the Accrington destination indicator boxes and the transfer of the roof-mounted headlights to the standard L & CBER position in the centre of the dash. By 1936 their Accrington red and cream livery had been replaced by the now standard L & CBER green and cream; two years later the original seats were removed and rattan seats from the withdrawn 1907 cars fitted in their place. Seating capacity in this form was forty. In 1952–3 all five cars were equipped with self-aligning trolley-heads bought as spares from Birmingham, and with Dunlopillo seat cushions from the same source. No 5 also had a change of motors, the new ones coming from one of the ex-Bournemouth cars.

All five survived until closure.

Nos 6–15

The second batch of secondhand cars were acquired from Bournemouth in 1936 and were a rather mixed lot in all, comprising ten passenger cars and one works car; the passenger

Page 145: The L & CBER: *(above)* No 6 (ex-Bournemouth) and successor (ex-East Kent) outside Rhos Depot. Scrapping in background. *(D. W. K. Jones)*; *(below)* the former reserved section through Bod a Fon Fields with Nant y Gamar Road in foreground and the Little Orme in the background, 1974.

cars were of two separate designs though all were basically open-top, double-deck bogie vehicles.

The first design was represented by No 6 (Bournemouth 85), built by the United Electric Car Co in 1914. It had elliptically-shaped end platforms with vestibules that dated from 1920. The bogies were Brill 22E maximum-traction trucks with a Westinghouse 226N motor in each, giving a total of 80hp. Other electrical equipment was also by Westinghouse while the lifeguards were by Hudson-Browning. Three braking systems were fitted: hand wheel, magnetic and hand track. After arriving at Llandudno the old motors were replaced with BTH GE249 pattern, these in turn being replaced in 1953 by two of the Dick, Kerr 40hp motors obtained from Birmingham along with the accompanying gears, wheels and axles. No 6 remained in service until closure and, as described in the previous chapter, has by good fortune been preserved. (Comparative dimensions are given below.)

The second design was made up of two distinct groups in terms of age. All were from Brush, the older group being built in 1921 and numbered (Bournemouth numbers in brackets): 9 (108), 10 (103), 11 (95) and 13 (112). They were generally similar to the vestibuled No 6 in design but with slightly longer semi-circular end platforms. Trucks were again Brill 22E but this time BTH electrical equipment was installed: B49 motors and B49CC controllers. Again the motors developed 40hp – as did their Llandudno replacements, BTH GE249 units. In 1953 all four received the same treatment as No 6 and were fitted with ex-Birmingham motors, gears, wheels and axles. Brakes were similar to those on No 6. Nos 9 and 10 were scrapped in January 1956 while Nos 11 and 13 survived until closure.

The younger group of the second design comprised five cars, built by Brush in 1924–6, and numbered (Bournemouth numbers in brackets): 7 (115), 8 (116), 12 (128), 14 (121) and 15 (114). Trucks were again Brill 22E only this time they arrived with Metrovick MV104 motors (again of 40hp) and Metrovick controllers. Upon arrival BTH GE249 motors were fitted and in 1953 Nos 8, 12 and 15 were equipped with ex-Birmingham equipment in a similar manner to Nos 6, 9, 10, 11 and 13. No 7 held the dubious honour of being Bournemouth's 'last car' while No 8 was of course later awarded a similar distinction on the L & CBER. All survived until the closure, then (except No 6) going the way of the rest for scrapping.

More detailed dimensions of the ex-Bournemouth passenger cars are given in the table below.

	No 6	*Nos 7–15*
Wheelbase: bogie	4ft 0in	4ft 0in
Wheelbase: total	20ft 0in	20ft 0in
Length: over body	23ft 6in	23ft 6in
Length: overall	35ft 6in	36ft 6in
Width	6ft 4in	6ft 4in
Seating: upper deck	32	38
Seating: lower deck	30	30

Nos 23 and 24

The last two cars acquired by the L & CBER were ex-Darwen Nos 24 and 23, renumbered 23 and 24 respectively at Llandudno. They were modern closed, double-deck trams with transverse seating for fifty-six passengers and had been built in 1936–7 by the English Electric Co. Entry was through a centre entrance on each side; the single trolley was centrally mounted on the roof. The pair arrived at Llandudno in 1946 but trials over the tramway were delayed until late 1947 as the maximum-traction bogie trucks had to be sent to Burton-on-Trent for regauging from 4ft. Each car was powered by two 57hp English Electric motors and was equipped with English Electric/Dick, Kerr K33 type controllers. Other refinements were air hooters and air brakes.

The previous chapter has described how, on account of their 4ft gauge-designed superstructure, they were prohibited from working the more exposed stretches of the line; instead they were regularly used on shuttle services in Llandudno and Colwyn Bay until withdrawal took place in 1954. (They had in fact been withdrawn from the Llandudno local working some five years previously as the condition of sections of the track there was so bad that it was having a damaging effect upon the cars.)

Livery

All the secondhand cars were, sooner or later, repainted in the official 1933 livery which was basically: panels – green; framing – cream; roof – dark orange; underframes – dark brown; trucks and lifeguards – red oxide; fenders – black. Gold numbers were carried above the headlight in the centre of each dash. The company crest was displayed on each side of the body.

Indicators

The relevant notes given in the previous section apply to the secondhand as well as to the original stock though in the case of Nos 23 and 24 a slightly different arrangement was used. On these two cars the side destination indicators were not fitted; instead destination blinds were shown above the cab windows giving (for No 23) the Llandudno terminal points and (for No 24) those for Colwyn Bay.

OTHER CARS

Ex-Canvey Island cars

As has been mentioned in the previous chapter, the first cars to work on the L & CBER were a pair obtained in 1907 from the defunct Canvey Island Electric Tramways. They had been constructed in 1904 by Brush Electrical Engineering Co of Loughborough and were of a standard single-deck closed design. The 17ft long body (25ft 6in over fenders) was mounted on a single type A truck with 30in diameter wheels on a 6ft wheelbase. Seating was for up to twenty-six on longitudinal seats each side of the saloon.

When the Canvey Island venture ground to a halt in the same year that it had got underway – 1904 – the stock of four cars was returned to Brush, whence two were borrowed in January 1907 by Bruce Peebles for testing the Llandudno line so far constructed. Later the same year they were returned to their maker, never having been numbered or used in service at Llandudno. After standing in Brush's works yard for several years they were eventually broken up during World War I for re-usable components.

Works cars

During its life the L & CBER possessed two powered works cars. The first was originally built by Brush in 1901 for the Taunton & West Somerset Electric Railways & Tramways Co Ltd (later the Taunton Electric Traction Co Ltd). It was an open-top, double-deck, four-wheeled car with a 6ft 6in wheel-base. In 1905 it was sold (along with Taunton's other five original cars) to Leamington & Warwick Tramways. Here one of the six was renumbered and converted into a scrubber car. In 1930 it moved again, this time to Llandudno where it remained in use for six years before becoming, less running gear, a stores shed.

The line's second works car was obtained in 1936 to replace the one above and it possessed a somewhat similar history. It had begun life in 1901 as a G. F. Milnes product for the Poole & District Electric Traction Co (No 1), a double-deck, open-top, four wheeled car on a Brill 21E truck. In 1905 the car was acquired together with the P & DET by Bournemouth Corporation Tramways and renumbered 55. Wheelbase was 6ft, as was its width; length was 27ft 7in overall (16ft over the body). Controllers were BTH B18s and the motor G58s from the same firm; the lifeguards were by Tidswell. In 1921, while still at Bournemouth, No 55 was converted into a rail-grinder and the top deck removed – although a rather peculiar effect resulted from the fact that neither staircase was so treated! It came to Llandudno with the others purchased in 1936 and was given plain grey livery and the number 23. In 1947, after the arrival of the ex-Darwen cars, it was renumbered 23A.

In addition to these two cars the L & CBER also operated three non-powered vehicles: a tower wagon, a welding unit and a small trailer bogie for carrying rails (obtained from Coventry in 1941). These essential items of maintenance equipment were simply towed to wherever needed by a works car and then positioned manually.

9 Minor lines and major schemes

HARLECH TRAMWAY

Excluding the minature tramway at Rhyl described later in this chapter, the Harlech Tramway was the most minor of the North Wales tramways in every sense of the word. As well as being the shortest in length it was also the shortest in life-span; the track, believed to have been adapted from a neighbouring quarry line, was probably of a gauge in the region of 2ft. No technical details are known about this tramway – even the official name (if indeed it possessed one) has not yet been discovered – and consequently all the existing information is best presented in its original form. The four quotes given below represent (at the time of writing) the sum total of this information; the only other contemporary reference I have found is another newspaper item which merely duplicates some of the details.

> THE NARROW GUAGE [sic] RAILWAY. – The contract for this little railway, or rather tramway (as we understand the carriages are to be drawn by horses) has been let to Mr Godfrey Morten, of Tremadoc. The length, from the Cambrian Railway to the beach, will be six hundred yards, and by the terms of the contract it is to be finished by the middle of June, but the contractor hopes to have it finished a week or so before that time, so that the little line will be in full swing before the great influx of visitors has commenced. We understand that there is to be a refreshment-room at the beach end of the tramroad with bathing machines both for ladies and gentlemen, which will be under the management of Mr Lovegrove, of the Harlech Castle Hotel. The engineer is Mr Thomas

Roberts, of Portmadoc. The Harlech beach is noted for its hard sandy bottom, and if required, the line can be extended both ways along the beach without much expenditure beyond the cost of laying down sleepers and rails. Mr Samuel Holland, M.P. for Merionethshire, is defraying the cost of this venture. The first sod of the tramway was cut on Good Friday [19 April]. It has been suggested the water power now running to waste might be utilised to raise goods from the station to the town, thereby effecting a great saving besides being a great benefit to the poor horses now engaged in the work.

(*Caernarvon & Denbigh Herald* 27 April 1878)

THE TRAMWAY. – The permanent way is now finished, and has been handed over by the contractors to the proprietor. Mr Rees Evans builder, Harlech, is making the "rolling stock", and the inhabitants expect to see the thing in full operation in the course of a few days.

(*Caernarvon & Denbigh Herald* 29 June 1878)

[Harlech] beach, which is three-quarters of a mile from the town, is gained by a small tramcar, which commences to run at 7.30am and ceases at 8.30pm.

(*Postal Directory of Merioneth* 1886)

. . . the bathing beach can be approached by tram car from near the railway station; but in some summers the tramway has not been used.

(*Gossipping Guide* 1890)

The route of the tramway cannot be traced today with any degree of certainty; from the above quotes it seems that the line ran west or north-west from close to the station at the foot of the one-time seacliffs upon which the famous castle stands across the flat sandy land to the dunes fringing the beach. From here later extensions in both directions would have been possible. (The last sentence of the first quotation appears to be a plea for a funicular incline, similar to those worked by water power in slate quarries, up the steeply-sloping cliff upon which the town is built.)

Sometime during the 1880s the tramway ceased to run. The reason for its demise cannot even be guessed at; certainly it was one of Holland's less profitable ventures compared to his close involvement in the slate industry and the narrow gauge railways of the nearby region.

VORYD PARK TRAMWAY

In the early 1950s the coastal resort of Rhyl was host to the narrowest, shortest and most transient of all the North Wales lines – though the first two claims are not too surprising considering that it was a $\frac{1}{4}$ mile 15in gauge minature tramway laid in the Voryd Amusement Park! The equipment had begun life as a portable line for use at fetes and the like, built and operated by Mr C. W. Lane, a New Barnet engineer and manufacturer of battery-electric delivery vehicles. After three years' operation (including in 1951 trials on a short length of track at St Leonards on the south coast) a more permanent site was sought and in 1952 the Rhyl tramway was opened. The semi-permanent trackwork was laid with flat-bottom rails on wooden sleepers; the rail joints were welded to give a smoother and faster ride.

The line was single and stretched from the Promenade (West Parade) inland to Wellington Road where it turned sharply right, following the road westwards as far as the coach park. A short second road was provided at each terminus and at the Wellington Road curve was a two-track depot shed with space for four cars. The track was ballasted throughout except where it crossed the two entrances to the park from Wellington Road. Here it was paved and check rails laid to give a level roadway for pedestrians and coaches.

The tramway was worked by electricity supplied from a substation outside the depot fed from the town supply; a transformer-rectifier unit stepped-down the current to 60Vdc for the overhead wire. From the wire it was then collected by trolley poles and swivel heads on the two trams. The first of the original two cars was a $\frac{1}{3}$ scale model of L & CBER No 23, the ex-

Darwen car, with a centre entrance and straight staircases. Accommodation on the two decks was somewhat cramped! The body was mounted on two maximum-traction trucks each powered by a 1hp motor. The driving cab at each end was fitted with a series-parallel type controller. The car was constructed in 1948 and was followed in the next year by a model of Blackpool Corporation No 225. Mechanical and electrical equipment was similar to that of No 23. In 1952 a third car was built to handle the large volume of traffic met with at Rhyl; this was in the much-requested 'old tram' style and appeared as a four-wheeled double-deck open top car of a freelance Edwardian design. The interior bulkheads and ceiling were decorated with ornamental woodwork; seating inside was on longitudinal slatted seats while single transverse seats with a central gangway were provided on top. Numbered 3, it was more powerful than its predecessors with two 2¼hp motors. Contactor-type controllers with standard series-parallel control were fitted, together with an electrically operated emergency brake to back-up the usual hand operated mechanical type.

All three trams were provided with destination blinds with a choice of four possibilities: WELLINGTON ROAD, PROMENADE, DEPOT or RESERVED. Two were normally in service at any one time, providing a shuttle service backwards and forwards through the park. The fare of 4d single or 6d (2½p) return was collected by the driver who also acted as conductor.

At the end of the summer season (Whitsun – September) the cars were removed by lorry to Lane's Lancaster Electric Co premises at Barnet. It was fast becoming apparent that the concern was rapidly outgrowing the 'one-man hobby' stage and consequently a company was formed to carry on the operation under the name Modern Electric Tramways Ltd with Lane as managing director and chief engineer. A larger and better site was sought and found at Eastbourne whence the tramway moved in 1954, opening the following Whitsun on the wider gauge of 2ft. So ended the proud boast of running 'the only 15in gauge tramway in the world'; so too ended the only tramway that ever reached Rhyl (see below) after just two seasons' operation! With the closure of the line No 23 was sold and the other two cars – the single-deck open No 225 and the double-deck open top No 3 – regauged for use at Eastbourne, only to be sold later to an American purchaser.

After leaving Rhyl the tramway passes outside the scope of this book; to bring the story up to date it should be mentioned briefly that the Eastbourne line closed in September 1969 and moved to occupy part of the old London & South Western branch to Seaton in Devon. Services began here, on 2ft 9in gauge, in August 1970. This is mentioned because the tramway possesses some curious material links with another North Wales tramway – the L & CBER. With the adoption of 2ft gauge at Eastbourne it became possible for new trams to be constructed incorporating actual equipment obtained from scrapped 'full-size' cars. Thus Eastbourne cars Nos 2, 4, 6 and 7 incorporated, together with parts from other systems' trams, the following items:

No 6 (1956 New Barnet) Top deck seats and scroll work from L & CB No 8 (ex-Bournemouth). Headlamps, gongs, signal-bells and circuit-breakers from various other L & CB cars.

No 7 (1958 New Barnet) Top deck seats from the ex-Bournemouth L & CB cars. Headlamps, gongs, signal-bells and circuit-breakers from L & CB No 3 (ex-Accrington).

No 4 (1961 Eastbourne) Motorman's valves, air whistles, controllers and circuit-breakers from the ex-Darwen L & CB cars.

No 2 (1963 Eastbourne) Parts of L & CB cars used in the construction of bulkheads and sliding doors.

GREAT ORME CABINLIFT

Although not strictly speaking a tramway, but deserving mention for the sake of completeness, the Great Orme Cabinlift has latterly provided the Great Orme Tramway with a serious rival. Promoted in the late 1960s by the Llandudno Cabinlift Co Ltd (a company linked by common ownership with similar concerns at Alton Towers, Uttoxeter, and Trentham Gardens, Newcastle-under-Lyme), the scheme was at first refused planning permission from Caernarvonshire County Council but the

Page 155: (above) The Happy Valley terminus of the GOC, 1974; *(below)* the remains of the Beaumaris pier tramway, 1974.

promotors successfully appealed against this decision. It was constructed by Messrs Lycett of Tamworth, Staffs, civil engineering contractors, to the specifications of Mr J. Presland, the company's design engineer; the total cost of the installation was £120,000. The opening ceremony took place on Monday 30 June 1969 and was performed by Lord Mostyn.

The cableway commences at the lower terminal (135ft above sea level) on Camera Hill on the eastern edge of the Orme, immediately overlooking the Happy Valley open-air theatre. From here it extends in a straight line for one mile to the summit, 651ft, running roughly parallel to the upper section of the GOT. The steel running cable is a 10,750ft long loop supported on nine towers, the tallest of which is 80ft high. On the cable are forty-two closed four-seat cabins which complete the trip each way in 9min. The theoretical capacity of the cabinlift is 1,000 passengers an hour; 1974 fares were 55p single and 80p return for adults and 20p and 30p respectively for children. These are considerably higher than those charged on the GOT and it will take several years before the long-term effect – if any – of the cabinlift on the tramway is apparent.

PIER TRAMWAYS

Although North Wales possesses – and has possessed – a number of piers and jetties of different ages and lengths, only two ever sported pier tramways and neither of these progressed beyond the hand-propelled luggage line stage. The first was at Bangor and was opened with the pier on 14 May 1896 by Lord Penrhyn. Before 1896 the Anglesey ferrymen operated with small rowing boats from a short stone jetty; steamer passengers were taken from the jetty in similar boats at high tide or from the end of a treacherous $\frac{1}{4}$ mile iron grating at low tide. The new pier was built 100ft to the west of the old slipway by Alfred Thorne of Westminster, to the design of the firm's engineer, John J. Webster. The tender for construction was £14,475 but the total cost was nearer £17,000. The pier was built of iron and steel, 1,550ft long and 24ft wide (with wider bays) and photographs taken during its construction show a tramway down the centre. This contractor's line was incorporated into the decking when this was laid and according to the handbook issued at the time of the opening the 3ft gauge grooved rails 'run the entire length of the Pier, on to the landing stage, for the easy carrying of light merchandise'.

The pier was used by steamers from Liverpool and the North Wales coast; they were boarded via a floating stage at the end of the pier onto which the tramway actually ran by a flexible bridge. The baggage trucks used on the line were said to have been specially designed for the purpose (if this was indeed the case they must have been rather more elaborate than mere flat wagons) and were manhandled up and down the track, though, according to a contemporary guide to Bangor, the line 'may probably in the future be worked by electricity or other motive power'. This idea was taken up two years later when a scheme was privately and unsuccessfully promoted in 1898 for electrifying and extending the line through Bangor to the station to provide, in conjunction with a steamer ferry, a fast link between Beaumaris and the Chester-Holyhead railway. During World War I the pier was damaged by a cargo steamer which broke loose from nearby moorings and was repaired by the Royal Engineers; it is believed that the tramway was lifted then. Today no traces of it remain and the whole future of the pier is now in doubt.

Across the Menai Straits was a very similar pier line at Beaumaris. The original pier dated from 1846 but was extensively rebuilt in 1872 after suffering serious damage; further work was put in hand in 1895 to extend the structure and it is thought that the 2ft 6in gauge tramway, laid down the west side of the pier, was installed at this time. It probably ceased to see much use after World War I though most of the grooved rails remain, now purposeless relics of the vanished age of the pleasure steamer.

PROPOSED TRAMWAYS

Besides being rich in the character of its tramways actually built, North Wales also saw a number of fascinating schemes and proposals for lines which never got off – or rather, on – the ground. The various proposed extensions to the tramways that were constructed have been dealt with in the relevant preceeding chapters and pages; what remain to be covered are those other, isolated proposals for tramways to serve the communities of the region, ranging from the industrial townships in the east to the rural villages of the west. For the sake of convenience they will be described on the basis of five separate geographical areas: Deeside, the coast, Anglesey, Lleyn and Snowdonia.

Figures in parenthesis refer to the tramways on the map on this page.

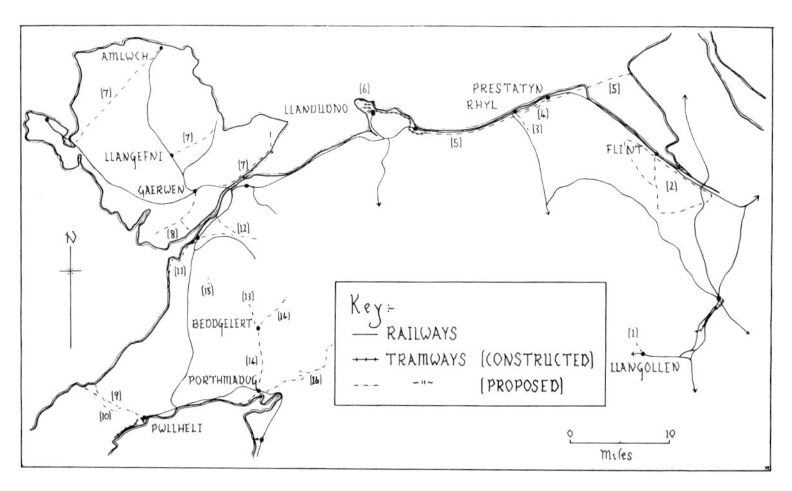

11 The proposed tramways of North Wales: see text for key to lines

Deeside

Like several of the schemes put forward for the other areas, the two proposals for tramways in the Deeside region never progressed beyond the first tentative stage of development; little concrete evidence exists with regard to routes, equipment and the like for either line. The first (1) can best be dealt with by quoting directly what was probably the sole newspaper reference to the proposal:

It is reported that a syndicate has been formed for the purpose of constructing electric cars to run between Llangollen and Vale Crucis Abbey. Last summer several Americans were at Llangollen, and it is believed that the proposed system is the outcome of the visit. The Americans also approached several of the proprietors of the flannel factories about Llangollen and Glyn with a view of purchasing the factories, but no agreement or sale has yet been effected.

(*North Wales Chronicle* 11 January 1902)

The second scheme (2) was assured of more solid backing. In June 1903 Holywell Rural District Council was informed of the proposal of a number of local gentlemen to apply for parliamentary powers to construct and operate some thirty miles of electric overhead tramways on a roughly circular route. The company's base was to be at Connah's Quay and from there the line was to go via Flint, Bagillt, Holywell, Mold, Buckley, Hawarden, Sandycroft and Queen's Ferry back to Connah's Quay. The system's one branch was to be from Flint to Northop. A meeting was held on Wednesday 14 October in Chester and several of those present subscribed towards the estimated capital of £20,000. A fifteen minute service was envisaged and 'heartiest approval' was extended from the local authorities. After that promising start the momentum appears to have been lost and no powers were ever granted for what would certainly have been a very useful and much-used line serving industrial Flintshire.

The coast

The major part of tramway promotional activity along the North Wales coast between the Dee and Bangor centred around Llandudno, Colwyn Bay and Rhyl; details of the schemes connecting the first two places have been covered in some depth in Chapter 7 in connection with the Llandudno & Colwyn Bay Electric Railway. There were however two tramways planned to serve Rhyl which were not intended as any part of a grand coastal line.

In 1883 application was made to the Board of Trade on

behalf of Messrs Archibald Fuller, F. C. Winby and C. A. Bury for a provisional order authorising construction of a 3ft 6in gauge tramway between Rhuddlan, Brynhedydd and Rhyl (3). Total length of the line was to be 2 miles 76 chains (all single except for 17 chains of double track) and the cost estimated at £3,500. Working was to be by animal or mechanical power. The application was successful and an Act of the same year to confirm certain Board of Trade Provisional Orders (46–7 Vic c133) included the officially entitled Rhyl, Voryd, and Plastirion Tramways. Despite this authorisation the project never became a reality.

The second scheme (4) was more ambitious, this time intended to join Rhyl with the neighbouring resort of Prestatyn. The idea of such a link, to be built under a light railway order, gained momentum during the late 1890s and in the last year of the decade Rhyl Urban District Council pledged its support to the promoters who had made the necessary application for such an order in November 1898. The order was granted on 3 April 1900, authorising the Rhyl & Prestatyn Light Railway Co Ltd to raise capital of £45,000 for the purpose of constructing a line along the centre and side of the road

> 3 miles 5 furlongs and 6.18 chains or thereabouts in length wholly situate in the County of Flint commencing in the parish of Rhyl at a point in the centre of the road known as East Parade . . . proceeding thence along the centre of East Parade Plastirion Parade and Marine Drive . . . Tynewydd Road . . . thence proceeding for a distance of 3457 yards or thereabouts through lands belonging now or recently to the trustees of the late Emmanuel Bradley . . . Captain Conwy and the London and North Western Railway Company . . . thence along the Rhyl and Prestatyn Road . . . terminating in the parish of Prestatyn at the point of intersection of High Street and Sandy Lane.

The gauge permitted for this line was also 3ft 6in and provision was made in the order for using electric traction. Time allowed for the completion of the work was three years.

In the month following the issuing of the order the promoters applied for a second order, this time to authorise various extensions through the streets of Rhyl. The order was granted and issued on 7 December as the Rhyl and Prestatyn Light Railway (Extensions) Order, 1900. Eight separate street sections through the principal streets of Rhyl were authorised, totalling 1 mile 74.6 chains in length. At the same time the company's capital was increased by £30,000 but the extensions, like the main line, were never laid.

A third tramway scheme (5) was far grander in theory but far less likely to have succeeded in practice. It was reported in the local press in September 1903 that an electric light railway was being planned from West Kirby on the Wirral across the Dee and on to Rhyl, Colwyn Bay and Llandudno. It is not surprising to learn that the plan, which would have required a bridge or causeway and bridge at least four miles long across the Dee estuary, was never heard of again!

Moving westwards along the coast, the next scheme met with (6) involved the use of the Great Orme Drive. (Brief details of the history of this road have been given in Chapter 5.) Completed in 1879 and purchased by the council in 1897, it was a toll road 4 miles 130 yards long around the Great Orme, hanging to the cliff face. The distance between the two toll gates across the peninsular was less than 1½ miles. Even before it had been fully opened suggestions were being made to replace the road with a tramway. One such proposal came from the writer of a letter to the *Caernarvon & Denbigh Herald* of 21 August 1875 who claimed that the tram fare would be in the region of only 3d – compared with the sum of 5s (25p) charged by the fly drivers who drove people round the Orme. The suggestion though remained just a suggestion for a quarter of a century until, during the protracted birth of the L & CBER, Llandudno UDC decided to investigate the idea more fully. The general purposes committee submitted a report by the engineer Mr E. Paley Stephenson to the council in November 1901; the report was a detailed study for what would be known as the Great Orme's Head Marine Drive Tramway. It was to follow the plan of the proposed Llandudno-Colwyn Bay line in that it would be a

3ft 6in gauge electric overhead tramway; on the Marine Drive section of the route from the Happy Valley Lodge on the eastern side of the Orme to the Penmorfa Lodge on the west the line was to run 3ft from the kerb along the landward side of the road while between the two entrances to the Marine Drive two alternative routes were considered. The first was via Abbey Road, West Parade, Conway Crescent, Gloddaeth Street and North Parade; the second was via Abbey Road, Tudnor Street, Church Walks and North Parade. The first route was the preferred one of the two as a possible agreement could then be arranged with the Llandudno & Colwyn Bay promoters for common running over this section. The second route would be more costly to operate and would also raise more opposition from residents.

Construction of the line would have entailed the removal of about 1,350 cubic yards of rock from the drive as the road was discovered by Mr Stephenson to be narrower than the statutory 16ft in several places. The cost of construction was estimated at £34,000 for the first route and £35,000 for the second. A 15 minute service was envisaged running in an anti-clockwise direction round the headland with both open and closed cars and a fare of 6d (2½p).

It is tempting to speculate as to whether or not the tramway would still be with us today if it had been built – but it was not, killed by the reluctance of the council to begin a new tramway venture when it might well be called upon to complete the one already on its doorstep, opposition from Llandudno Pier Co who saw a possible loss in revenue and, one would imagine, similar opposition from the promoters of the Great Orme Tramway.

Anglesey

Anglesey was the scene, at the close of the nineteenth century, for a number of tramway proposals. There were several reasons for this rash of promotions, the two principal ones being the fact that railway communications came to a focus close to the Menai Strait, so making cross-island journeys somewhat circuitous, and the fact that the pronounced flatness of the island –

in vivid contrast to most of the rest of North Wales – would facilitate any light railway or tramway construction.

The first scheme (7) to be mooted was ambitious. In March 1897 the local press carried reports that a London-based syndicate, represented by Mr Theo Rowlands of Llanerchymedd, planned to spend no less than £140,000 on electric light railways that would in effect fill in the gaps left on the map of Anglesey by the main London & North Western Railway line to Holyhead and its branches. Three separate lines in all were proposed: standard gauge lines from Amlwch in the north-east across to the LNWR at Valley in the south-west and from Llangefni in the centre of the island to Pentraeth and Red Wharf Bay on the eastern coast; the third line was to be narrow gauge (2ft 6in), from Llanfair P.G. (to use the usual abbreviation for the artificially named Llanfairpwllgwyngyllgogerychwyrndrobwllllantysiliogogogoch) along the shore of the Menai Strait (though not actually at sea level) to Beaumaris, then inland to the village of Llangoed. A narrow gauge was presumably chosen on account of the shelving and indented nature of this part of the coastline.

A less ambitious scheme was adopted two years later (8) in May 1899 by Dwyran District Council for a 3ft gauge electric overhead light railway from Gaerwen on the LNWR to Brynsiencyn, Dwyran and Newborough in the southern corner of the island. Just before reaching Dwyran a short branch was to lead down to Tal y Foel on the Menai Strait. Further extensions were envisaged 'as soon as practicable' to Bodorgan on the LNWR and to Llanddwyn Bay. The cost of the first stage, excluding the purchase of the necessary land, was put at £30,000. Where the roads were wide enough (which, judging by present-day standards, would have been nowhere!) the track would occupy the roadway, otherwise it was to have its own reservation.

While the above system was being planned, part of the first set of proposals was being arduously promoted, the rest of the 1897 scheme having been abandoned. In April 1898 the Light Railway Commissioners met in Beaumaris to consider an application for an electric tramway from Llanfair P.G. to Beaumaris (by far the largest settlement on Anglesey without rail connection). The former extension to Llangoed had also been abandoned and this left a total proposed length for the 2ft 6in line – virtually the narrowest practical gauge – of 6½ miles. The roadside course followed what is now the A5 to Menai Bridge and then the A545 to Beaumaris. The meeting was adjourned to 19 May 1898 and evidence was heard from the county council in favour of, and from the local landowners against, the proposed line. The commissioners did not deliver their decision until some seven months later. It was unfavourable:

> the narrowness and difficult features of the road, coupled with the strong opposition of those living along it, had compelled them reluctantly to come to the decision that they could not be justified in submitting to the Board of Trade an order authorising the construction of the line.
>
> (*North Wales Chronicle* 7 January 1899)

So that was that. The 'strong opposition' of those living along the route was only to be expected – the coastal stretch between Menai Bridge and Beaumaris was (and still is) very much the 'select' residential area of the island, commanding magnificent views of the straits and the mountains of Snowdonia beyond.

Lleyn

At the turn of the century the idea of a rail link across Lleyn was already some sixty years old: Porth Dynllaen, across the peninsular from Pwllheli, had been one of the main contenders for the British mainland railway terminus on the mail route to Ireland in the mid-1830s. After the choice of Holyhead for the honour and the construction of the railway to that port, Porth Dynllaen faded into obscurity, briefly re-emerging in the 1860s as part of the grandiose vision of the Potteries, Shrewsbury & North Wales Railway. It was not until the 1880s that the rising fortunes of Pwllheli led to agitation for a railway link across this comparatively populous part of Lleyn. Thus in 1884 the Porth Dinlleyn Railway Co obtained its Act for the purpose of building such a link. Three years later it drew up an agreement for the Cambrian Railways to work the line, ignoring such minor details as the complete absence of the line in question! In 1888 a time extension for construction was sought and obtained; when this elapsed with still no work implemented the Cambrian was approached for financial help but without success. A further time extension to 1895 was secured but it proved a pointless move and this too lapsed with nothing to show for it.

Undeterred by this setback its supporters carried the project into the twentieth century still very much alive. In 1900 a change of tactics resulted from a more realistic view of the situation in financial terms and a light railway order was applied for. This application – by a Manchester syndicate – was for $6\frac{1}{2}$ miles of standard gauge electric light railway from Pwllheli Station to Morfa Nefyn, just east of Porth Dynllaen. The application was rejected by the commissioners, mainly because of opposition from local landowners and the failure to secure a Treasury grant for construction, and in the following year the idea of a parliamentary bill was once again toyed with, but dropped.

Again the interested parties refused to give up and rallied their forces for another try at a light railway order. By 1903 matters were coming to a head. By the summer Pwllheli Town Council had pledged unanimous support for the scheme (though not if it was to interfere with the streets of the town). On Thursday 1 October 1903 the public enquiry was held into the application made by the North Wales & District Light Railway & Electric Power Syndicate for an order to authorise the construction of the Pwllheli, Nevin & Portinlleyn Light Railway (these being contemporary English spellings). The application was for a main line of 10 miles 4 furlongs length from Pwllheli to Porth Dynllaen and a branch of 1 mile 6 furlongs at the northern end to Nefyn. The main line (10) was rather more circuitous than that of the 1900 proposal (9).

Traction was to be by electricity and the gauge standard to provide a physical link with the Cambrian. Envisaged traffic consisted of commodities associated with the agricultural, slate and fishing industries, plus of course passengers. Estimated cost was £170,000 – hopefully to be supplied by grants from the

Treasury, Pwllheli Town Council and Caernarvonshire Town Council. It was stated that the Cambrian was willing to work the line in return for 70% of the receipts.

At the inquiry difficulties were met with over the question of the exact route to be taken through the streets of Pwllheli in order to reach the station and the proceedings were adjourned. The differences between the promoters and the town council were never overcome and by March 1904 the whole scheme was at a standstill. In June 1906 the Cambrian commenced a motorbus service across the peninsular from Pwllheli to the various villages and any lingering hopes of a tramway were well and truly killed.

Proposed in 1899 was a line on the very fringe of Lleyn: this was to be a tramway to Dinas Dinlle, a bathing-spot 6½ miles south-west from Caernarvon. The tramway, which would have run along the foreshore for most of the way, would undoubtably have proved popular with holidaymakers and those seeking a day out but again the project was one that never really got started, one of the obstacles preventing it from doing so being the difficulty of reaching a suitable terminus in, or close to, Caernarvon (11).

Snowdonia

It would be no exaggeration to say that Snowdonia probably had more narrow gauge and light railways both proposed and constructed than any other comparable area of Great Britain. The railway history of this region has been adequately covered elsewhere; only those proposed lines which cross the ill-defined border between 'light railway' and 'tramway' are relevant to this present study. In chronological order of proposal they were as follows.

In June 1899 Caernarvonshire Town Council had plans prepared for a light railway between the village of Ebenezer and Caernarvon (about six miles) and an alternative scheme for a similar line between Penisarwaun and Port Dinorwic via Bethel was also planned (12). At the same time the council pledged its support to Dwyran District Council's light railway proposals on Anglesey (see above), stating that it would be willing to co-operate in any scheme 'calculated to improve traffic between Anglesey and Caernarvon' (*Chronicle* 10 June 1899). It is not difficult to see why this scheme never progressed beyond this first expression of intent. Penisarwaun was close to the LNWR branch from Caernarvon to Llanberis and it hard to imagine just what sort of traffic was envisaged from there or Ebenezer (later swallowed up by the village of Deiniolen) to Port Dinorwic since the major industry in the area was the Dinorwic Quarry – and both slate and workers were carried by the 4ft gauge Padarn Railway (including workers who crossed every week from Anglesey). And unless exorbitantly expensive earthworks were constructed, the line to Port Dinorwic would have had to terminate, like the Padarn Railway, high above the village. Presumably with hopes centred on passenger traffic between Ebenezer and its surroundings and Caernarvon, the plan lingered on throughout 1899. In November of that year Gwyrfai District Council authorised the spending of £100 by Llanddeiniolen Parish Council on the preliminaries connected with the proposed construction of a light railway from Ebenezer to Caernarvon 'or any other neighbouring town agreed upon' (*Chronicle* 25 November 1899). After that the whole scheme joined the south-west Anglesey plan in oblivion – though it progressed as far as an inspection of the Isle of Man tramways by members of Caernarvon Town Council in 1901.

The early years of the twentieth century saw a host of light railway schemes in Snowdonia to 'open up' the area. Even though several of these projects proposed using electric traction (a result of the building of local power stations) all were in fact narrow gauge railway rather than tramway proposals and as such are outside the scope of this book. Thus the North Wales Narrow Gauge Railways (Beddgelert Light Railway Extension) Light Railway Order 1900 authorising the extension (13) of the NWNGR line from Snowdon to Beddgelert permitted the line to be worked electrically; the Portmadoc, Beddgelert and South Snowdon Railway Act of 1901 authorised the construction of an electric railway from Black Rock Sands, Morfa Bychan, through Portmadoc to Beddgelert (using part of the course of the former Croesor slate tramroad) then up the Vale of Gwynant to a power station situated on the shore of Llyn Gwynant (14); a light railway order of 1905 gave further powers to the NWNGR, this time for the working of the Moel Tryfan branch (15) as an electric line and in 1906 the Festiniog Railway (16) considered using tramcars for passengers and locomotives for slate trains, both electrically powered; this handful of examples should suffice to show how quickly the idea of electric traction was seized, promoted with enthusiasm, then dropped.

Appendices

1: THE NORTH WALES TRAMWAYS

Tramway	*Gauge*	*First section opened*	*Last section closed*	*Total length**	*Traction*
Wrexham	3ft 0in	1876	1901	3 miles	Horse
Harlech	2ft?	1878	1880s	¼ mile	Horse
Pwllheli & Llanbedrog	3ft 0in	1896	1927	4 miles	Horse
Pwllheli Corporation	2ft 6in	1899	1919	½ mile	Horse
Great Orme	3ft 6in	1902	—	1 mile	Cable
Wrexham & District	3ft 6in	1903	1927	4½ miles	Electric
Llandudno & Colwyn Bay	3ft 6in	1907	1956	8¼ miles	Electric
Voryd Park	1ft 3in	1952	1954	¼ mile	Electric

** to nearest ¼ mile*

2: OPENING & CLOSURE DATES

	Date	*Tramway*	*Line opened*	*Line closed*
1876	1 November	WD	Johnstown—Ruabon Rd	
	November	WD	Ruabon Rd—Ruthin Rd	
1878	July?	H	Station—beach	
1880s		H		Total
1896	1 August	WE	West End-Carreg y Defaid	
1897	July?	P & L	Cardiff Rd—West End; Carreg y Defaid—Llanbedrog	
1899	26 April	WD		Total
	24 July	PC	Station—Victoria Parade	
1902	31 July	GO	Victoria Hotel—Halfway	
1903	4 April	W & D	Wrexham General—Johnstown	
	Spring	W & D	Turf Hotel—Wrexham General	
	8 July	GO	Halfway—Summit	
1904		W & D	Johnstown—Ponciau	
1907	19 October	L & CB	West Shore—Rhos Depot	
1908	7 June	L & CB	Rhos Depot—Station Rd	
1915	26 March	L & CB	Station Rd—Old Colwyn	
1917		L & CB		Dale St—Gloddaeth Av

Date		*Tramway*	*Line opened*	*Line closed*
1919	Summer	PC		Total
1927	31 March	W & D		Total
	28 October	P & L		Total
1930	21 September	L & CB		Greenfield Rd —Old Colwyn
1932	23 August	GO		Total
1934	17 May	GO	Both sections reopened	
1952	Summer	VP	Voryd Park	
1954	Summer	VP		Total
1956	24 March	L & CB		Total

GO — *Great Orme Tramway*
H — *Harlech Tramway*
L & CB — *Llandudno & Colwyn Bay Electric Railway*
P & L — *Pwllheli & Llanbedrog Tramway*
PC — *Pwllheli Corporation Tramways*
VP — *Voryd Park Miniature Tramway*
WD — *Wrexham District Tramways*
W & D — *Wrexham & District Electric Tramways*
WE — *West End Tramway*

3: WREXHAM & DISTRICT FLEET LIST

No	*Built*	*Builder*	*Type*	*Withdrawn*	*Remarks*
1	1903	Brush	4wt	1927	
2	1903	Brush	4wt	1927	
3	1903	Brush	4wt	1927	
4	1903	Brush	4wt	1927	
5	1903	Brush	4wt	1927	
6	1903	Brush	4wt	1927	Body preserved
7	1903	Brush	4wt	1927	
8	1903	Brush	4wt	1927	
9	1903	Brush	4wt	1927	'Last tram'
10	1903	Brush	4wt	1927	

All double-deck, open top

4wt – four-wheeled truck

4: WREXHAM & DISTRICT SAMPLE RETURNS

Year	*Traffic receipts*	*Working expenses*	*Car mileage*	*Passengers*
1904	£ 5,659	£ 3,906	133,469	847,760
1905	5,280	4,103	141,447	855,600
1910	5,108	4,075	143,427	852,770
1913	7,241	5,097	155,632	1,227,330
1914	17,678	13,378	*	*
1915	16,252	12,429	*	*

Year	*Traffic receipts*	*Working expenses*	*Car mileage*	*Passengers*
1920	£ 46,991	£ 38,769	135,385	1,035,850
1925	56,066	42,048	139,729	812,733
1926	69,749	54,018	104,107	402,831
1927	84,487	62,845	20,722	74,903

* *figures not available*
From 1914 onwards traffic receipts and working expenses include the bus accounts

5: GREAT ORME FLEET LIST

No	*Built*	*Builder*	*Type*	*Withdrawn*	*Remarks*
1	1902	HN	4wt	?	Freight 'jockey' car
2	1902	HN	4wt	?	Freight 'jockey' car
3	1902	HN	4wt	?	Freight 'jockey' car
4	1902	HN	8wb	–	Passenger car, lower section
5	1902	HN	8wb	–	Passenger car, lower section
6	1903	HN	8wb	–	Passenger car, upper section
7	1903	HN	8wb	–	Passenger car, upper section

4wt – four-wheeled truck
8wb – eight-wheeled bogie
HN – Hurst, Nelson & Co

6: LLANDUDNO & COLWYN BAY FLEET LIST

Original stock

No	*Built*	*Builder*	*Type*	*Withdrawn*	*Remarks*
1	1907	MRC & W	8wb	1932/3	
2	1907	MRC & W	8wb	1932/3	
3	1907	MRC & W	8wb	1932/3	
4	1907	MRC & W	8wb	1932/3	
5	1907	MRC & W	8wb	1932/3	
6	1907	MRC & W	8wb	1945	Renumbered 16 in 1936
7	1907	MRC & W	8wb	1936	
8	1907	MRC & W	8wb	1936	
9	1907	MRC & W	8wb	1936	
10	1907	MRC & W	8wb	1937	Renumbered 19 in 1936
11	1907	MRC & W	8wb	1956	Renumbered 18 in 1936
12	1907	MRC & W	8wb	1936	
13	1907	MRC & W	8wb	1936	
14	1907	MRC & W	8wb	1956	Renumbered 17 in 1936
15	1909	UEC	4wt	1936	Broken-up 1941
16	1909	UEC	4wt	1936	Broken-up 1941
17	1909	UEC	4wt	1936	Broken-up 1941
18	1909	UEC	4wt	1936	Broken-up 1941

All single-deck saloons

Original stock

No	*Built*	*Builder*	*Type*	*Withdrawn*	*Remarks*
19	1920	EE	8wb	1956	Briefly renumbered 23 in 1937
20	1920	EE	8wb	1956	
21	1920	EE	8wb	1956	
22	1920	EE	8wb	1956	

All toast-racks

Ex-Accrington stock

No	*Built*	*Builder*	*Type*	*Acquired*	*Withdrawn*	*Remarks*
1	1920-2	Brush	8wb	1932/3	1956	Ex-Accrington 28
2	1920-2	Brush	8wb	1932/3	1956	Ex-Accrington 29
3	1920-2	Brush	8wb	1932/3	1956	Ex-Accrington 30
4	1920-2	Brush	8wb	1932/3	1956	Ex-Accrington 31
5	1920-2	Brush	8wb	1932/3	1956	Ex Accrington 32

All single-deck saloons

Ex-Bournemouth stock

No	*Built*	*Builder*	*Type*	*Acquired*	*Withdrawn*	*Remarks*
6	1914	UEC	8wb	1936	1956	Preserved; ex-85
7	1924-6	Brush	8wb	1936	1956	Ex-115
8	1924-6	Brush	8wb	1936	1956	'Last tram'; ex-116
9	1921	Brush	8wb	1936	1956	Ex-108
10	1921	Brush	8wb	1936	1956	Ex-103
11	1921	Brush	8wb	1936	1956	Ex-95
12	1924-6	Brush	8wb	1936	1956	Ex-128
13	1921	Brush	8wb	1936	1956	Ex-112
14	1924-6	Brush	8wb	1936	1956	Ex-121
15	1924-6	Brush	8wb	1936	1956	Ex-114

All double-deck, open top

Ex-Darwen stock

No	*Built*	*Builder*	*Type*	*Acquired*	*Withdrawn*	*Remarks*
23	1936/7	EE	8wb	1946	1954	Ex-Darwen 24
24	1936/7	EE	8wb	1946	1954	Ex-Darwen 23

Both double-deck, closed

Works cars

No	*Built*	*Builder*	*Type*	*Acquired*	*Withdrawn*	*Remarks*
—	1901	Brush	4wt	1930	1936	Scrubber car; originally double-deck, open top; ex-Taunton and Leamington & Warwick

Works cars

No	*Built*	*Builder*	*Type*	*Acquired*	*Withdrawn*	*Remarks*
23	1901	Milnes	4wt	1936	1956	Rail-grinder; originally double-deck, open top; ex-Poole and Bournemouth 55; renumbered 23A in 1947

4wt – *four-wheeled truck*
8wb – *eight-wheeled bogie*
EE – *English Electric Co*
MRC & W – *Midland Railway Carriage & Wagon Co*
UEC – *United Electric Car Co*

7: L & CBER SAMPLE RETURNS

Year	*Traffic receipts*	*Working expenses*	*Car mileage*	*Passengers*
1908	£12,068	£ 6,454	185,082	1,060,281
1909	14,272	8,306	247,843	1,356,323
1911	15,359	8,001	267,141	1,505,603
1913	17,710	8,395	272,908	1,768,142
1915	17,482	9,219	288,152	2,061,106
1917	18,061	10,011	267,449	2,050,089
1919	30,633	22,770	282,070	2,879,636
1921	38,035	27,417	264,164	2,327,337
1923	35,351	27,354	361,588	2,444,170
1925	28,029	23,451	410,803	2,353,966
1927	22,505	21,662	428,353	2,049,657
1929	20,910	20,773	464,472	2,436,826
1931	14,635	14,840	406,533	1,779,505
1933	19,700	16,718	437,698	2,399,831
1935	19,341	17,446	428,207	2,485,782
1937	20,086	16,152	417,992	2,625,259
1939	20,056	16,286	405,793	2,657,586

8: LLANDUDNO & COLWYN BAY BUSES

Between 1955 and 1959 the L & CBER Co purchased a total of eighteen double-deck buses: fourteen were obtained from Southdown and two each from Newcastle and East Kent operators. Not all of them saw service for one was used only for driver training and another as a source of spares. Chassis manufacturers were Leyland, Guy and Daimler while bodywork was by Park Royal, Weymann or Northern Coach Builders. Garaging and maintenance was carried out at the former tram depot.

The original service ran at 10 minute intervals, later changed to 15 minutes as a result of the Suez crisis, later still to 20 minutes; the buses closely followed the tramway route except at the reserved sections and when track removals were in progress.

Livery was maroon and cream – hence the local epithet of 'the red buses'.

Bibliography & Sources

BOOKS

Anderson, R. C. *Great Orme Railway* (1969)

——. *Llandudno & Colwyn Bay Electric Railway Limited.* (Exeter, 1968)

Bett, W. H. & Gillham, J. C. *Great British Tramway Networks.* (1962)

Boylett, L. J. *Eastbourne Tramways.* (Hampton Court, 1963)

Christiensen, R. & Miller, R. W. *The Cambrian Railways.* Vol 2. (Newton Abbot, 1969)

Crosland-Taylor, W. J. *Crosville: The Sowing and the Harvest.* (Liverpool, 1948)

Day, J. R. *More Unusual Railways.* (1960)

Dodd, A. H. (ed). *A History of Wrexham.* (Wrexham, 1957)

Klapper, C. *The Golden Age of Tramways.* (Newton Abbot, 1974)

Lawson, R. & Morris, G. C. J. *Llandudno & Colwyn Bay Electric Railway.* (1956)

Tucker, N. *Colwyn Bay: its origin and growth.* (Colwyn Bay, 1953)

PERIODICALS

Modern Tramway
Railway Magazine
Trams
Tramway and Railway World

NEWSPAPERS

Caernarvon & Denbigh Herald
Liverpool Post
Llandudno Advertiser
North Wales Chronicle
North Wales Pioneer
North Wales Weekly News
Rhos Herald

OTHER SOURCES

Manual of Electrical Undertakings (various years); contemporary guide books and published souvenirs; all relevant statutory instruments including Acts of Parliament, Light Railway Orders and Board of Trade Provisional Orders; reports of the Light Railway Commissioners; Pwllheli Borough Council Minute Books; timetables; OS maps; sundry items of ephemeral material relating to the background, setting and history of each line described.

Index

Plate pages are given in *italic*